CHANGING THE FILIPINO MIND

A Spark of Renaissance to help Change the Culture

Marq Martin

Business Training Philippines | Cebu City

CHANGING THE FILIPINO MIND

BY
MARQ MARTIN

ISBN: 978-1-69196660-8

First printing edition 2019.

Business Training Philippines
Unit 211 Century Plaza, Juan Osmena St.
Cebu City, Cebu 6000

marqmartin.com

Contents

Changing the *Filipino* Mind

PROLOGUE

This is a handbook for every Filipino to ultimately become happy, healthy, and wealthy. It is to change the mentality of many Filipinos who have not been able to achieve their goals, who live in misery, and who think that being poor is their destiny. It is OK if you were born poor, you had no choice. That's life. If you die poor, then that is your decision which eventually becomes your own fault. This book is made for you to die *rich*.

When I decided to write this book, I observed that a lot of Filipinos are poor because they have negative beliefs about money and about rich people. A lot of them blame the rich for having all the money or blame the government for the economy. Maybe they are right or maybe not; all I know is if you continuously blame others, you have *less* power to make changes in your life. You will learn why when you read through this book.

I have been to many places in the Philippines; poor neighborhoods, the richest houses of Cebu, and far away provinces that people live surrounded by trees. I have talked to the people about any subject they want to talk about, they ask me any question they want, and I answer them *honestly*. From what I noticed a lot of poor are happy or content with being poor. If they live in a Provincial area, I guess being surrounded by nature, in some ways, is a natural luxury.

Even though a lot of poor have accepted being poor, it does not mean they are happy all the time. The common problem of being poor is since they have no money; they have to borrow or ask people for money. If they need to go to the hospital and cannot afford it, they become stressed out in times where money becomes a *necessity*. I think they are OK with being labeled as poor. But I know if I gave them a choice to receive 1 peso, or P1,000,000.00, they would choose the million and be very satisfied with the choice.

Although they would have the million pesos, it would be gone within a year because they *continuously* label themselves as poor. If your self-image is being poor, you will never be able to hold on to a million pesos. I will explain more about this in the book, this is why it is about changing the *Filipino* mind, because yourself image is in your mind. Whatever you hold in your mind, will manifest itself into outer experiences.

This is also for people with messed up personalities. Even the richest people I've met or people just well off in a way, have messed up personalities. They're unable to see the soul in every person and God's creations. They live unhealthy lives and spend much of their money on food, vacations then hospital bills. There's a lot of people who might have money, but are unhappy and unhealthy.

A lot of people who are also spiritual are somewhat broke and bitter at everyone who isn't "Enlightened" like them. They haven't understood that even money also has a spiritual essence as all things doo. Even a rock has a spiritual essence in some way. Everything thing and everyone is part and connected as one. The biggest problem with people who value, or want to look spiritual, is they think money has no spiritual essence.

I guess this is for every Filipino out there all over the world. The things I've learned and experienced over the years of studying and practicing personal development, from NLP, Universal Laws, Subconscious Programming, all the Religious, Spiritual and Philosophy books. I've read all the success and self help classics, as well as business classics. Not only that, I've applied what works for me in my life. I'll share with you what I hope works for you, and I hope your life changes for the better after readings this book

Acknowledgements

Go thank Mike Perez for helping edit the book. He started it in Cebu but left for Jersey City. Shout out to everyone from Jersey City! Everyone that I work with in Business training Philippines and my office furniture company in Cebu. I want to thank my family, my Dad in heaven, my mom, sister, and two brothers. Also, my wife and kids, just letting you all know I love you.

Might as well give love to everyone I ever knew and met, all the people who think of me time to time. Much love to all of God's creations, even in other planets and life forms. Got to continuously give and create love energy. Only two things to keep in your mind and heart, everything you love, and your goals. Anything or anyone less should never enter your thoughts.

Also, would like to thank the people who showed interest in my book when I was preselling it. For some reason I postponed the publication and just became a lazy writer, but still working hard in everything else, from consulting, corporate training, the furniture business, and other business ventures.

For all the people who are reading this book, thanks for picking up a copy and actually reading it. I haven't been writing books as much as I should, but this book has made me realize I can write several books a year. I also realized writing books is something I really love to do. It puts me in the zone where I find cell phone notifications a distraction. It eliminates my urge to check social media.

It makes me feel happy to write this book for you. I hope you really benefit from it, learn and apply the knowledge in your life. You can also teach others what you've learned and hopefully the knowledge brings changes in your life in the most positive way possible.

Gratitude

If you get nothing from this book but living in gratitude, you will live a beautiful life. When you are grateful you are directly *connected to God* in the closest way possible. The feeling of Gratitude changes your energy level. It is a positive energy level. Gratitude will make you attract more of what you are grateful for. When you catch yourself complaining, always replace it with gratitude affirmations.

I noticed here in the Philippines; people believe they have bragging rights to complain about something negative. They have battles in conversations in the office. One person complains that she fell off a motorcycle over the weekend, and someone else jumps in and says they got hit by a car 5 years earlier. It is like “Mine is worse”. One person says that he hates his work, his co-worker says “I hate this work more!”.

Avoid toxic people, and avoid being a toxic person. A toxic person is someone who brings your energy level down when you talk to them. They might be the ones that play the victim and they need advice because they are worried or sad about something, they can be just argumentative, someone that always looks for the opposite of whatever you say. They definitely are those who complain and criticize everyone and everything to make them feel superior and the other party inferior.

We will cover more about those who complain and criticize for now. *Avoid* them. When people complain around you, they eat your positive energy, the lower it. You get more of what you pay attention to. So, when you are paying attention to a complainer and are not well trained in positive thinking, you might agree with everything they say. You might also be polite and pretend to agree. Either way, just being next to them will make feel negative. So, the first step is to avoid them at all cost.

The opposite of a complainer is someone that is content and satisfied with life. You can only be satisfied with life if you are grateful for what you already have. When you start understanding The Law of Attraction, you will know that whatever you focus on multiplies. So, when you are grateful every moment of the day, more people, events and (great)circumstances will come into your life that you are already grateful for.

Become grateful. What you focus on with feeling will expand and multiply. When you focus on the thorns in life, things that hurt, people that hurt you, situations that are painful, you get more of the same. When you focus on roses, things that went right, people that your thankful for, and all the good in life, you will receive an abundance of that as well.

Notice the people you consider to be happy. Some characteristics might be they do not complain much, they are kind, which means they act with love, they are always ready to give, and they wish the best for you and they have positive expectations. They are grateful and they usually do not have major relationship problems. They have a good relationship with their loved ones, people in general, money, and most importantly, *God.* People who think good thoughts always live good lives.

People who are grateful always have it better than those who complain. Way better! So, one way for you to begin being grateful is to create your affirmations that help you feel grateful. You can start with “Thank You”. Saying thank you repeatedly for 10 minutes any time of the day is something that will help you to generate the feeling of gratitude. You can say "Thank you God for my abundance of blessings". This affirmation is great because you are indeed thankful and you are also paying attention that you have an abundance.

The key to seeing results when it comes being grateful is to be grateful most of your day and Not just for 5 minutes in the day. Every time you notice yourself complaining, start saying your gratitude affirmations. Try to be grateful the whole morning. While you have your coffee be grateful. Be grateful for who you are with in the morning. When you start paying attention to those who are idiots, stop focusing on them and be grateful about something special.

Gratitude is one of the greatest feelings in the world, it is so great that when you feel it, you get more of what you are feeling from what is outside of you. "*As within, so without*" The quality of your environment and all life events existed within you first. There is nothing outside of you that didn't come from inside of you. When you are angry inside, you potentially make other people angry. So, when you are grateful, you also make other people grateful for you. What you give to the world, you receive sometimes 10-fold; therefore, gratitude is an act of giving to God. As you give to God, God will give back to you.

Give back to all those that ever helped you in life. Think back as far back as you can think, when you were a child, be grateful for all the people that took care of you, any aunts or uncles that gave you candy or a nice birthday present, or took you on a trip, be grateful for your siblings, be grateful for everything good in high school, all the teachers that were good to you, all the bosses you had that were good to you. There must be hundreds even thousands of things you should be grateful for. **Be *so* grateful that you shed tears.**

Be in a Continuous Feeling of Gratitude. Start when you first wake up, keep going all day. You might have ups and downs, but just remember: when the downs start to show up, use your gratitude affirmations. Stay thankful and *feel* thankful all throughout the day. Your gratitude should be continuous, which means unending. Whatever happens, stay with the feeling of gratitude. Whoever you deal with feel grateful for them, even if you know they are not perfect. Let nothing stop you from your Continuous Feeling of Gratitude.

No Criticizing

What I noticed in the workplace, in schools, from neighbors, basically everywhere that people know each other, a lot of groups in the Philippines unfortunately criticize each other. Even in the jeep, I am uncertain of the ratio but I am very sure people in the jeep criticize each other silently sitting across each other. This does them no good.

When it comes to criticizing, you cannot give to anyone what you do not hold within you. If I give you a gift and the other people refuse to accept or acknowledge it, then I keep that gift. I criticize you and you do not even know I am criticizing you, then I keep that criticism. Even if you know I criticized you, I keep that negative energy because it came from me.

Try for 30 days not criticizing anyone-- the outcome, along with benefits, are tremendous. One benefit is you will have more confidence. From what I noticed, the people who criticize others are 99.99% of 100% are the most insecure. I know this guy that just makes fun of everyone and everything. On his Facebook he makes fun of whoever is the laughing stock of the moment. It might range from a poor kid, ugly old lady, homosexuals. It is just pathetic. Then when I run into him, he asks the dumbest questions out of insecurity. He asks like "Is my hair OK?" "What do you think of my shirt?". Then if I say something that makes him feel insecure, he will overreact.

People that fear criticism the most, are the ones criticizing the most. The average person still fears to talk in public, to talk on video, to get out their comfort zone or try to reach a goal because they fear criticism. They fear criticism because when they walk in the mall, they criticize the fat lady with her belly is showing, they criticize the girl who has really nice hair but is butt ugly when she turns around.

They criticize the Jollibee cashier as the idiot who got their order wrong. When you react to people negatively then you also become a walking pile of negative energy. For example, if someone makes a mistake and gives you a burger instead of chicken, you have several ways to react. You can yell and insult, which will come back and hurt you spiritually. Or you can accept that it is meant to happen and just eat the chicken, not letting the cashier know she made a mistake.

For me, I always ask "*What did I do to attract this*?". For everything, bad or good that appears in my life, but I investigate on it deeply only if it is bad that I may figure out the *root cause.* In order for you to change any problem in life you have to find the root cause. It will always be in your inner deepest thoughts and beliefs, or whether you helped or harmed others.

Again, just try at least for 30 days. You can replace looking for negative things to say to people to saying something good about them, or do not say anything at all. I am sure you have those negative friends or people you know who can find something negative about how you look the first 5 seconds they see you. So, they can say “You gained weight”, or “What are you wearing? It looks funny” or “I heard you fell in Zumba class”.

Some people think criticizing others makes them look better cause “At least that wasn't me” or “At least I'm not living that guy's life”. Yeah it should make you feel good to compare yourself to others who have it worse than you. It is still certainly not a good route to take. You should compare yourself only to yourself.

My suggestion is to practice the art of acceptance. Be like water. Just accept everyone and everything as they are. If you do not like what that guy is wearing, do not pay attention to it. Do not talk about it. When you talk about it, you connect to that “*I don't like*” energy, and attract more of that. When you see a crazy naked man or woman walking in the street, do not tap the person you are next to so they can also take a look, but rather allow everyone to be as they are; so, the world will allow you to be who you are.

Criticizing is not allowing. When you criticize yourself, you are not allowing yourself to be who you are. You do the same when you criticize others, it just depends how they choose to respond. You should *never* criticize yourself. Begin with *not* criticizing others, and include yourself in the challenge. Do not criticize yourself and do not criticize others. Criticism is a common blockage that creates common people to live common lives. Criticism has common people afraid to risk, because fear of criticism to take a chance or made the change to live higher standards.

Fall in Love with Yourself

There are plenty of people that will criticize you. You have been criticized all your life day in and day out. After you leave your best friend's party, I am sure someone there is criticizing you. Why be the one to criticize yourself? In order for you to feel deserving of the good things in life, you have to feel good about yourself.

There are a few parts of you that we can touch on. The first part is yourself image. Most of the people in the world have a self-image created by what people say about them and what they say about themselves. You have a self-image right now. The question is, did *you* create yourself image?

Creating yourself image is something that I think most Filipino people do not do. They allow others to tell them they are not good dancers, they are not good at math. They allow others to tell them what they are good at and not good at. It is time to have control of yourself image. If you been raised to be told that business is too risky and it is better to have a high paying job, then when you start having inner urges to start a business, you probably will not go for it, even though you calculated everything and you are sure your business will succeed, you might not take the risk.

One way to change your image is through affirmations, repeated phrases that you say over and over until it becomes ingrained in your subconscious mind. If you want to start your business, but you do not see yourself as a business owner. Keep repeating "*I am a successful business owner*". Do this first thing in the morning, and during your free time throughout the day. It is especially good to do it while you are waiting in line. Instead of complaining about the wait, you can just say affirmations and day dream of your success.

Just fall in love with yourself. List all the things that you love about yourself; this will help you discover yourself worth. You will feel worthy of what you have, who you are, and know that you are worthy of receiving more. The more you feel good about yourself, the better you perform, and the better you will attract in your life. If you hate yourself, you will attract others that hate themselves. If you love yourself, you will attract other people that love themselves.

Faith and Trust in God and People

In order for you to receive the things that you want, you need to have faith that you will get what you want in life. There are a lot of people in the Philippines that go to church and pray and have faith in God. Yet there are also those who go to church and do not have faith in God and only attend for a sense of familiarity.

In order for you to be happy with your life, *faith & trust* is one of the necessary ingredients. It is really important to trust and have faith in people too. Have faith that they are doing their best with what they have. Have faith that people around you have good intentions. Trust that everyone around you will help you achieve your goals.

See the Good Side of Everyone

Average people think highly of themselves and lowly of other people. This is not good. When you think negatively towards others you are actually seeing what you do not like about yourself and noticing it in other people. When you say that someone is a show off, you are actually reminding yourself that you are in fact, also a show off. You cannot see in others what you do not have in yourself.

Arrogant people see the best in themselves in the worst of others. Confident people see the best in themselves and the best in others. It is good to remind yourself that there is a good side to everyone. Maybe someone is a killer and a drug dealer, but they also love their mother, wife and children. On the surface yes, this killer is bad for society, but when he goes home, he is loved, and he also loves.

When you choose to see the best in the world, you receive the best in the world. Noticing the best in other people and talking about the best parts of them, can *dramatically change* what appears in your life. Try for 1 week or maybe for the rest of your life? Only pay attention to the best part of other people. You will notice that you'll have less stress, and have positive energy.

Every day we notice that people are constantly saying bad things about other people. This goes most especially in the Filipino workplace-- in call centers! Every time I go to I.T. Park for dinner or lunch, there are a lot of workers who are complaining about other co-workers, and talking trash about callers. Anytime you say bad things about others, you connect with them.

Here is a solution for people who work in a job where they deal with negative people all the time. Anytime someone is negative towards you, never talk about that person. The more you talk about that person, the more you connect with them spiritually, and you ingrain an emotional connection with them that is negative. So then next time you have lunch, never talk about angry callers, never talk about rude supervisors. Talk about something good, that you want to spiritually connect with. Talk about your plans. Low people talk trash talk other people, average people talk about themselves, successful people talk about their plans.

When you encounter negative people, you might mention the negative experience, but never dwell or talk too long about it. If you really need to talk about it, just talk about the negative person once. Do not be those people that every time they run into a common friend; they talk trash about that person to try to convince the common friend not to like them also. I doubt doing this will change anything.

Do not let a negative person be worth your breath. The next time you have dinner with your loved ones or friends, do not mention any negative people. No talk of any negative event. Only say the good things going on, or plans you have for the future. Anytime you talk about a problem, it should only be 10% of your time and effort, while 90% should be finding *the solution.*

Thinking of negative people is also bad, because you allow them to take up space in your head. The time and energy thinking about negative people is the same time and energy you could be using to think about your goals, about an optimistic future, and people you love. Your thoughts connect you with what you think about. So only think of the best people, and see only the best in others.

See the Best in You

The possibility of you being born as a human is miracle. It is easier to win the lottery 1,000,000 times than to be born as a human. You are here for a reason that is *good.* Never believe that you are living your life to suffer. Know that there *is* a special reason your here. Right now, if you do not know your purpose in life, I will give you a temporary purpose. Right now, your purpose in life is to figure out what your purpose in life is.

There is this verse from a rapper named Lupe Fiasco. It's kind of represents how a lot of people who are depressed and sad feel like. "*All you see is all my flights, all I see is all my falls. All you see is all my rights, all I see is all my wrongs. All I hear is all my demons, even through your applause.*" Even the rich and famous commit suicide from depression. The reason is, no matter how good their life is, they only see the bad parts of it.

It is time for change. The average person sees the good and bad in themselves throughout the day. It is important to know what bad characteristic traits you have, as well as what bad habits are holding you back. The 90/10 rule should be applied to this, which is to spend 90% of your time turning the bad parts of you into good parts. Many people spend 90% of the time repeating the problem, but not much time finding a solution.

In order for you to even know the best part of who you are I suggest to write down the best parts of who you are. What are you *proud* of about yourself? What are you *good* at? What can you *do better* than anyone else? When it comes to work or career, what makes *you irreplaceable*? Whatever it is that makes you irreplaceable, you should be spending much of your time on it.

Another exercise that you can do to love yourself more is to repeat the affirmation "*I love myself*". There's a lot of silly thoughts if someone catches you doing this next exercise, but it's really effective and uplifting. Try looking in the mirror, look at yourself eye to eye. Then keep on repeating "*I love you*" or "*I love myself*". Send love energy to yourself.

Common blockages that may appear when you try to

increase the love you have for yourself may be unable to forgive yourself for something, guilt, self-criticism, and ashamed of something. The best thing you can do is to forgive yourself for any limitations or mistakes you might have made. Forgive others who might be involved in it. As for criticism, be consciously aware anytime you start to criticize yourself, replace criticism with self-praise.

Self-praise; complement yourself every chance you get. This will increase your self-confidence and it will make you love yourself more. Anytime you finish something on your to do list or achieve a goal, say something good about yourself! As for me, since I am writing this book, I tell myself I am doing a good job when I hit a milestone. When I achieve business success, I tell myself what a good job I did and compliment myself on my skills. I also have mini-celebrations like take the staff out for lunch or reward them with going to the beach.

A lot of the times, its negative self-talk that makes people hate themselves. They call themselves stupid, useless, ugly, or better off dead. There is a lot of negative self-talk in the average person day in and day out. It is time to replace negative self-talk with positive praising of what is good about you and complementing yourself. If you are noticing the good in other people, the good in your favorite celebrity, you owe it to yourself to see *the good in you.*

Be your own best friend. You should be the number one fan of you. Say good things to yourself and always let your internal dialog have positive expectations, like "*Today is going to be a great day!*" "*I feel like a lot of good things will happen today*". What you pay attention to grows. Pay attention to what is good about you and expect good things to come.

Good Vibes from Good Food

When was the last time you ate lechon or any kind of pig? Probably less than 24 hours ago. We are a country that really loves pig. Nothing wrong with it, but pig has the lowest vibrational frequency when it comes to food. It means it is not something that can increase your happiness. Also, as vegetarians probably told you before, when you eat an animal, their emotions get transferred to your body. Most animals we eat are basically born in prison and live in misery.

The best food that can give you good vibes are green leafy foods, vegetables, fruits, and cacao. I am not saying stop eating pig, just become more aware of the benefits of vegetables, and how your diet affects your happiness level. The more you eat food that is ultimately good for your vibrational frequency the better your mood, and the better things you attract into your life.

In order for you to make good decisions in life you also need to have a healthy brain. For most Filipinos, I think we eat too much white rice. White rice is not good for the brain. Sugar is not good for the brain, and too much mercury is bad. Too much fried food is also bad. It is important to eat lean, clean and green which means good food for your health would be chicken tinola with a lot of kamungay, and just one cup of rice.

One thing that I also noticed with Filipinos, more with the lesser income or people not from the city, is that they are not open minded to eating salad. When I was working in an office, the workers would call me a goat for eating lettuce and tomato salad. Several times I was even asked "You can eat that without cooking it?". The new generation, upper class, and people who been around the city are open to it, but probably will not eat it daily. Even recently the old helper jokingly said I am a goat, because I was eating salad. Maybe you can try eating salad in front of some maids or factory workers, and see how they react.

Eating healthy is important because of course health is wealth. Also, when it comes to your ability to create capital, and have money, your health is the number one factor. When you are able to eat healthy, without much exercise you can still remain healthy. It is way better if you exercise though. Just keep in mind the food you eat affects your level of happiness.

Importance of Exercise

Some people said if you want to get into self-development or positive thinking, just exercise. This is true. The benefits of exercise are plenty. There are physical benefits which means you will have more energy and eventually become strong. You will build confidence with your new body, more attractive physical appearance. The greatest benefit is that it makes you happy and makes you think positive.

As for me, I grew up as a negative thinker, because of many reasons. I know for a fact if I do not exercise, I will be grumpy all the time, and will not be totally happy. A lot of people get out of depression just by exercising on a regular basis. So much easier to think positive when you exercise. You will also be way more productive at work. Your focus, memory will increase, and you will find yourself making faster and better-quality decisions from critical thinking.

When it comes to excuses not to exercise Filipinos give the same response as other countries I believe. They say it is too expensive, they do not have the time, and the major one, it is tiring. They say what good is it if I exercise because I love eating rice and Jollibee? Maybe it's time to find an excuse to exercise. Knowing itis extremely beneficial and life changing, better to stop having reason not to exercise, and ask yourself *why I will* exercise?

Exercising in the start of your day is the best time to exercise. Dwayne Johnson "*The Rock*" wakes up 3 hours before any call time to work out. Barrack Obama and Michelle Obama wakes up 4am and workout. By the time they get to work, they have more energy because oxygen has been distributed throughout their bodies. Their mind is sharper, they think more clearly, and are in a better mood. They go to work with an aura that uplifts people, they are positive energy givers.

Working out is in the routine for most successful and happy people. If you want to be successful and happy, workout. I see a lot of middle age and older overweight people in the gym all the time. A lot of them are in the gym because the doctor told them if they don't work out, they'll get a heart attack, or their diabetes will get worse. They're working out after they spent money at the hospital.

I always say it's better to invest in the gym then he hospital. I'm sure there's a public track somewhere you can run in your city or town. If your excuse is the money then invest in the cheaper gyms. There's P500 a month gym popping up everywhere. Your P500 peso a month investment can save you from a P50,000 hospital bill. They even have P10 or P50 Zumba classes. It's even free in some malls. Sweat that toxic out daily if possible.

Yoga

The Philippines is starting to have a lot of yoga classes

everywhere. I been doing yoga for maybe 18 years on and off. The great benefits of yoga for me is the mental benefit. They put you in all kinds of uncomfortable poses and your job is to focus on breath and clearing your thoughts. So, in life, if you have difficult situations you are able to handle them more calmly and with a clear head. It is also good for sweating out the toxic in your organs. A lot of the poses benefit your internal organs. The saltiest sweat I get is from yoga. This means toxic is coming out my body. To many people's surprise I'm also a Yoga Teacher. I have about 5 or 6 classes per week.

Lifting weights

It is kind of weird sometimes, the mentality of some Filipinos when it comes to guys with muscles. The skinny guys always try to say that guys with muscles are "small" in the bedroom. This is not true. Working out and lifting weights will actually make you "bigger" in the bedroom. Not sure where that theory came from.

Lifting weights is beneficial for men and women. If you want to see the fastest results on your body, you should be lifting weights. Your mind will also benefit in ways that it will have oxygen, and it improves your will power. Many muscular men I know from the gym are usually happier, they laugh a lot, and are more confident.

Aerobics

Aerobics exercises like running and walking is winning the battle when people ask what type of workout is the most beneficial for the brain. Walking is really good for the mind as long as you're thinking good thoughts. Sulvitor Ambulando means the problem was solved by walking. When I run or walk in the morning as a workout, I feel more confident about the day. I already have it planned in my head, and I practice positive self-talk, which makes me feel good about myself before the day even starts. Out of all the workouts, start with running or walking before having breakfast, and notice an increase in the quality of your thoughts.

Never Depend on Others for Happiness

It is *your* responsibility to make yourself happy. No one else. Everyone else will be an addition on to your happiness. It is one of the saddest things in the world when you depend on other people to treat you well or be nice to you, just for you to be happy. Like a housewife that tells her husband "*Because you didn't kiss me goodbye in the morning, it means you don't love me, now I'm sad for the whole day, in fact I'm mad*!". You can still choose to be happy after someone says this to you.

Instead she can just say "Oh he didn't kiss me goodbye, OK, maybe he forgot. I'll just think and do things that make me happy.". When I say never depend on others for happiness it means, you should be happy inside all the time. You should be having beautiful conversations with yourself, your internal dialog should be words that lead to happiness.

The more you do things that make you unhappy, the more unhappy you will be. So, it makes sense to stop doing things that make you unhappy. Does it not? Now that we know one of the things that cause us to be unhappy, we should know what to do to make us happy. Like, if you do not like your job and it makes you unhappy, then find another job, or start a business that makes you happy.

Another way to find your way to happiness, is to write down everything that makes you happy so you know what it is. You can write spending time with your family, singing, doing a certain activity like exercising, writing, reading, having coffee with your best friend at a coffee shop. Just write anything and everything that make you happy. Then spend as much time doing these things.

Once you begin to learn how to master the art and science of being happy, you will never end up in an environment that makes you unhappy, and never come across a person that makes you unhappy. Imagine, Victor Frankl was captured by Nazi's and torched, but he said he has more freedom than any of the soldiers torturing him, because he knew that he was in total control of his thoughts. When you are able to control your ability to make yourself happy, and control your reaction to everything, nothing can disturb your inner peace, nothing can make you unhappy.

What you pay attention to grows so when you put most of your attention into things that make you happy, or thoughts that make you happy, then your mind will pay less attention to things that make you unhappy. The more you watch the news or look at Social Media Posts that are sad and make you angry, the more unhappy you will be. The more you pay attention to sad things, the sadder you will become.

Again, focus *less* on what makes you unhappy, and more on what makes you happy. Practice conscious decision making. One thing that I noticed about people is they have a list of things that make them unhappy, even me, but I decided to change my reaction. Like I used to get angry when workers make stupid mistakes. Mistakes that can be easily avoided. Now I choose not to react with anger but find a way to correct them, avoid the same mistake happening again, without anyone's feelings getting hurt.

Some people have a long list. "I *hate* people who wear socks with sandals, I *hate* men who wear rompers, I *hate* homo-sexualism, I *hate* this politician, I *hate* when people use beauty mode, *I get mad* when someone posts a picture with their car just to show it off, *I get mad* when people post sad stuff on Facebook. I *hate* anyone that doesn't believe in Jesus." The Jesus thing or religious thing kind of separates people. So, **get rid** of the list you have, because you are making yourself *un*happy. Get rid of the list of things that you hate or get you mad, replace it with a list of things that make you happy.

Since I am mostly an auditory thinker, which means a big part of my thoughts are in words, less pictures, I always use affirmations to change my mood. I say "*I feel happy, healthy and wealthy*" repeatedly to change how I feel. I say "I feel happy!". You can go as far as repeating "*Everything in my life makes me feel happy*" and as long as you continue to feel that way inside, everything outside will make you feel happy. As within so without.

Finding Your Purpose

To reinforce how important this is, if you haven't found your purpose, your purpose is to figure out your purpose. When you figure out your purpose you have one less thing to worry about in life. You also will feel a sense of certainty, like you know what you're doing is the right thing. Your purpose should be something bigger than you, it should be something that serves as many people as possible, or it can be to help one person or company that serves a lot of people.

Maslow Said something like your purpose should be to do something that brings out your highest potential. What is something that brings out your highest potential? My purpose is to help make the Philippines become a first world nation. So, I am bringing out my highest potential in business skills and creativity. In short, I will provide jobs, send kids to school with my charity, and write books and do seminars that help Filipinos become successful.

One of the ways to figure out your purpose is to first get rid of the idea of limitation. Like "It's impossible to be one of the top singers in the world". It actually is not, Charisse did it when she was 11 years old. It took a lot of hard work, practice, and developing her innate desire to reach her goals. So, get rid of all ideas of limitations and impossibilities. Second one is to know what you *love* doing. When you were a kid what did you love doing? What were you dreaming of doing when you were young? What is your greatest talent or talents? If it is drawing, sharpen your skills in designing and do not say "but, but...." If it's writing then write. If you think you are not good enough, get better. Spend an hour a day learning, practicing, and getting better. If you do this every day, you will gain the competence and confidence to be anything you want to be.

The worst way to find your purpose is listening to other people. When someone tells you that you should be an engineer, even though deep inside you are not sure what you want to be yet. When you are not sure what you want to be in life, don't let other people tell you what you should be. You can put suggestions in consideration, but don't follow anyone's suggestion on your purpose just because they said it, no matter who they are in your life.

Go inside and listen to your intuition, know your deepest desires and go for what you want in life. Better yet, what change do you want in the world, your city, or country? Do not just wait for someone to make the change, like Gandhi said, "*Be the change you wish to see in the world*". Make a plan, do some research, take some steps on the things you want to change in the world.

If you know you are talented at one thing or a few things, go for it. I believe most people are multi-talented. People can be good writers and singers. They can be athletic and a genius, you can be like me and Leonardo Da Vinci. You can be Renaissance Men and Women. If your purpose is to express multiple talents and inspire others to do the same, then do it.

Achieving Goals to Feel Happy

Another way to be happy, maybe one of the best ways is to achieve goals. Achieving goals should be a source of happiness for everyone. If you had a goal to have a new car and you got one, wouldn't that make you happy? If you wanted to lose weight and have the body you always wanted, wouldn't that make you happy?

I think it is safe to say that a lot of people in the Philippines do not set clear goals. They might have wishes or "Maybe one day" vague goals. A lot of them have this "*I want to achieve this.... but it's impossible*". Achieving goals is something that can benefit you, people you love, and whoever else may be involved.

So much about having the thing that you want. Let's say a financial goal to have P10,000,000 in cash. This is a good goal to have. Let's say you're only making P25,000 a month now. To achieve this big goal, you would have to change so many things about you. Starting with the way you think. You would have to get rid of your limiting beliefs, especially about money. You would have to increase your income, increase sales if you have a business, improve your management ability. So much about you would have to change.

Change is the only thing that's certain in life. The only way you can achieve goals is to become a better person. You're always better after achieving a goal, than before achieving a goal. As for me, I'm a writer, so finishing this book is my goal. After finishing this book, I will have increased my confidence that I know I can write good books (hoping you think it's a good book), and my ability to write books will improve. In order for me to write this book I had to be a writer in myself image, do what a writer does, which is write. From these two steps alone, I will have my book. During the writing process I am happy in daily progress, and after the writing process I am happy with daily sales.

Set goals that make you feel happy during the process. It is good if it makes you happy, but it doesn't have to make you happy all the time, because behind every achievement there is always pain. Even *Michael Jordan* and the greatest athletes do not enjoy every part of practice. There will be hell that you may have to go through-- just go through it, God will help you get through it. If it does not kill you it will make you stronger, if you make mistakes, it will make you wiser.

Keep in your mind that every goal achieved brings happiness. If you are happy during the process, it is fulfillment of purpose. *Manny Pacquiao* has a simple formula that works every time. He figured this out naturally. He said he sets a goal, makes a strategy to achieve it, and then disciplines himself to follow the strategy. This is so good! Many people set goals, change goals, do *not* have a strategy, do *not* have discipline.

Jack Canfield does the 5 things principle-- where he just lists 5 things, he can do every day to achieve his goal. When he had a goal to be a best-selling author, he had the discipline to do at least 5 things that moved him forward. He might not have enjoyed doing some of the 5 things, but he knew that achieving his goal will bring in more happiness in his life.

So, start making a list of goals you want to achieve, and make sure that every day you are making progress towards your goals. Notice a transformation that will take place daily. A metamorphosis, caterpillar to butterfly, Egg to Dragon. Oh, by the way if you achieve your goal and you are not as happy as you thought you will be, make another goal achieve it, another goal and achieve it, and so forth. Then you *will realize* it is not much about having the goal, it is being the person who is able to achieve that goal that brings happiness.

Core Beliefs that Make or Break Your Happiness

What you believe is true. If you believe that people are generally good, then you will experience being good to you. If you believe that you are not good at remembering people's names, then you won't even make an effort to remember people's names. When it comes to happiness, you have inside you a certain ideal of what your life would be like if you are happy.

One of the worst beliefs you can believe is that "*One day I'll be happy*". One of these days when I have my perfect partner, I'll be happy. When I finally get a job at the call center, I'll be happy. Believing you will be happy because of external things is a negative belief. It is time to dig into what are the beliefs that you believe that make you unhappy? Write down all negative beliefs that make you unhappy so you know what they are.

Also, everyone has rules that make them happy. Like just now, I was writing this book and I was not able to meet with one of my business associates. This person got angry because it is her rule that if you are late, she will be angry. I think this is true for most people. Since we do not want to be like most people, Let's eliminate this rule. Let's turn it into, if someone is late or does not show up, then I have time to read a book, I can say affirmations, I can practice day dreaming about the things I want. I can plan something and forecast my week let's make this rule now, that if someone is late, or doesn't show up for a meeting at a coffee shop, I will do something productive.

When you believe that everyone in the world is against you then. How in the world can you be happy? Believing that everyone's in it for themselves, or people are out to scam you will make you fearful and make yourself greedy. When you meet people, you'll have negative expectations and that brings unhappiness. It's time to pinpoint your low-quality beliefs, that is really a figment of your imagination ingrained in your subconscious.

Your Perception of the Universe

How you view the world to be, you will get in your life. If you think that the world is an evil place, you have fear of maybe getting robbed? You'll get more fearful events in your life. If you see the world as an evil place, then you will attract evil people in your life. When you see the world as a caring and loving place, you will attract caring and loving people and circumstances.

You receive what you choose to see in the world. What you pay attention to changes the molecules of that thing. If you pay attention to people that owe you money in a way that you are not sure if they will pay you back, or you think they are intentionally not going to pay you, then you will receive that type of energy, in other areas in your life as well.

Einstein said "*I think the most important question for humanity to ask is. Is this a friendly or Unfriendly Universe?*" When you begin to think of this world as a friendly world then you will notice a lot of nice people, and they will also notice your kindness. If you think everyone is just out to get what they can for themselves, then you'll notice that, and also subconsciously behave the same way.

Begin today to notice all the good things that world has ever given you. All the beautiful and wonderful experiences that you've experienced. Write down 100 things great about the world that you live in, about the people that live in the world. You can include how abundant the world is and how many people you know have pure hearts. How many people genuinely love you? How many people showed you kindness in your life? When you begin to notice how great the world is then you'll also experience great things.

Eliminate Your Dislikes

I may have touched up on this a bit already but this is really important to do. A lot of people think they're so special because they have a big list of things they dislike and nag about not liking this person, not liking their job, not liking tomatoes, or not liking the government. It's reasonable for people to dislike things, but they need to eliminate conversations about. It's a waste of time for the listener especially.

When you learn to focus only on people and experiences and things that you like. You really don't waste energy or thought on what you dislike. If you dislike something why would you keep it in your mind? You don't like the neighbor, why would you keep on thinking how much you do not like the neighbor? Why do you have one-hour conversations with people about how much you don't like your neighbor?

From learning about all the things, I know, I don't dislike anyone. I just accept people as they are and let them be. From what I noticed, when I meet people in social events, I can tell who dislikes me. One of the biggest reasons is because I achieved what they can't even imagine. They might feel less than me so they look for every flaw that they can and talk to people about any flaw or mistakes I made. Worst of all when people dislike you, they will just assume negative things or intentions that are not true.

Avoid talking to people about "*Maybe his intention was to rip you off.... Maybe this, maybe that. Maybe he's cheating on you. Maybe that girl has a sugar daddy, that's why she has that car.*". Avoid assuming the worse in people you dislike. When you start assuming negative things about people, it is a total waste of time, and also it brings you in a lower energy level.

Here is how to get rid of your dislikes. Write down all the things and people that you dislike. You might put on this list things like the way jeepney drivers drive, that pimple face short girl in the office, the guy in the gym that thinks he is so cool, or people that cut you in line. What is that too with cutting? People here just try to cut you in line like it is a tradition. Just write them all down.

If your list of dislikes is long, then you're most likely a negative person, and you focus on negative things a lot of times. Your life is probably not as good as you want it to be. Knowing this about yourself, is good, because now you can change. For each item on the list, write down something good that you like that is in the same polarity. For example, if you don't like Xander Ford, list down a celebrity that you do like. If you do not like cheese, write down that you like fried chicken. This way when you start focusing on something you dislike, you get triggered to not focus on the negative and focus on the positive.

God in Everyone's Eyes

Now, we touched a bit on seeing the good side of everyone. It is time to go a bit deeper and understand that God is in everyone's eyes. This is taught in all religions possibly? Practiced only by a *few* people in the world. God is in the eyes of the rich man, the beggar, the people in jail, the cashier, the monkey, the whales, the sea turtles, the wind, the clouds, the stars and planets unknown. *God* is in everything and everyone.

Some not so smart person when I said something about God in my poetry book, she said "*My God or your God*?" I do not know how some preachers brainwash people to point out anyone who does not believe what they believe as evil. "*This group is evil, that group is evil*!" I do not know why they do this --maybe to get more members or sales tactic? To convert more people? In reality, pointing out evil in others shows that there is evil in you. Again, when you point out evil, it shows there is evil in you.

When you can come to an understanding that God is in everyone's eyes you will begin to be more cautious when you interact with people, animals, or anything. Understanding that God is in everything takes conscious awareness at first until it becomes ingrained as part of your beliefs. Claiming that people are evil and treating them badly has a negative effect, because any negative act towards another person will always have a negative effect.

For me I always have sympathy for street kids. People say that the government should help them, or charities should find a better way to help them. Yes, these opinions might be true. As one person, I give them big amounts for them, when they ask me for money. Because God is in them.

I get criticized for doing this, but I also influenced others to do the same and see what effects it might have in their life. I give P100 on average when a street kid asks me for money. If I know there's an adult supervising them to ask for money then I will not give them. It is like organized begging. Maybe I am not seeing God in their eyes in this way. One of the principles of giving is, it is OK to give as long as you do *not* feel ripped off. When I give to organized beggars, I feel ripped off, so I only give to kids who are so desperate in life they need to ask strangers for money.

Put yourself in the slippers of these kids, cause a lot of them don't have shoes. Some don't even have slippers. Imagine you are a kid living in a fly-infested place, it stinks like fish, poo or whatever nasty smell it smells like in those squatter areas. You have no parents, you live with your aunt, she has no job, she is an on-call laundry lady who gets P250 a day *if* she has work. As of now she has no money to buy food.

You need money to buy food. People in your neighborhood

also have the same problem. What resources do you have to buy food? You could dig in the garbage for food. Maybe there is no food there today. So, you walk 1 hour to place where people have money they can spare. You do not know about any government agency or charity that might give you food, you're only 6 years old. You also do not know much cause your aunt does not have enough money to send you to school. You feel helpless, and all you know is poverty and misery.

These kids do not know where their next meal will come from. Their only happiness is playing throw the slipper with their friends. The majority of their days is feeling worthless, and unsure of the future. Here I come driving by and I hit a stop light. You try to sing a song to me and ask for money. While you get rejected by most cars, you might get bread from some, you might get 5 pesos here and there. When you knock on my window and I give you P500. The most money you ever got. How good would you feel?

Every time I give a kid P500 for them is like winning the lottery, and they get a feeling of abundance. I also feel good because I made someone else feel good. The *karmic effect* is also good because from my experience good things always happen to me. Some good things that might happen if you do this is the money you gave will come back multiplied. The feeling you gave of happiness comes back to you, because not only can he eat, he can play video games. Something that rich kids can play anytime they want. The amount of gratitude that kid feels, you will feel also. Plus, if you did a bad deed, bad might not come back to you, because the good deed *overrode* that bad deed effects

That is just one out of many parts where God is in everyone's eyes. Since God is in *everyone and everything,* you should send love to all of God's creations and know that nothing is truly evil. Everything is just the way it is. Just by knowing that God is in everyone's eyes, you should make a change to give more love, have more mercy, help more people. If you do not, the next time you ask for help, God *will remember* the people you refused to help, and give you the feeling you gave them.

Express Kindness Now

How often are you kind to other people? Is it a once in a while type of thing? I worked with this supervisor who was hardly ever kind, unless there was something in it for her. Regarding her work, it used to be a two people office it turned to an 8 people office, because her psychotic nature. All the workers hate her until this day. No one really wants to work. She lives a miserable and lonely life and it is all her fault. When you are mean to others, the world will be a mean place to live.

Before I had this type of knowledge, I used to be rude to people, insulting, made people cry, etc. if I was in a bad mood, I would end up putting other people in bad moods. I would run into people with bad moods and we would express our bad mood together. Sooner or later, bad things would happen to me. I would not get things to go my way financially, I would have relationship problems, I also had low self-esteem and lack confidence, I would be in fear and worry, since I did something bad to others, I deserved bad things to happen to *me*.

When you are in a negative vibrational frequency you can only express negative things to other people. You cannot think anything good if you are feeling bad. All of your thoughts and ideas will be bad ideas when you are feeling angry. Do *not take action* if you are feeling negative emotions like rage, or revenge, or jealousy, or anger, because it will only come back to you.

One way for you to overcome this negative frequency is to do acts of kindness. Not fake acts of kindness that you do a fake smile to someone you hate. I mean real acts of kindness like helping someone who is poor, saying something nice to someone, comforting a friend who just got dumped. Higher levels of kindness can be volunteering, making your own charity, sending food or treats to people in jail, visiting an orphanage and even adopting a child.

Especially those who cannot have kids, but really want kids-- adopt a child, do an act of kindness that will bring you and someone else happiness for the rest of your life. The good karmic energy you get when you adopt a child is timeless. It is one of the greatest deeds you do, to be a parent to someone who does not have parents. Every child should have a parent, and will need them for a long time. Even some 40-year-olds *still* need their parents.

If you feel bad one of the short cuts to feeling good is to do a kind deed to others. This benefits the giver as much as the receiver. When you give kindness to others you increase your vibrational frequency to a higher level. It can be in a level of love, gratitude, sympathy, joy, or any other positive emotions. Kindness will only bring about good results in your life. You will never lose when you give kindness.

The Power of Good Deeds

For every action, there is an equal and opposite reaction. This is a true statement, it is fact in science and in spirit.

For every action you take will boomerang back to you. This is why the more good deeds you do, more good comes back to you. Some people might complain that they always do good deeds and nothing comes back to them. They should consider if they did the good deed with a good attitude and good intention.

Any good deed taken with a bad attitude will still have a good effect, but the attitude will still be a factor if you will receive good from the good deed you have done. If you are angry or feel forced to do a good deed, yes you will have benefits, but it is still going to be a coin flip on the quality of benefits you receive.

If you do good deeds with bad intentions, then you will get back to you the quality of your intention and will receive little goodness from the good deed. So, consider your intentions, make sure they are pure. Some people give to charity so people think they are a good person, others will give a woman gift, hoping they can get laid. Always consider the pureness of your intention when doing good deeds.

The true power of good deeds given with good intentions is something that will benefit all involved in this action. I look at good deeds and bad deeds as a math equation. The more you do good, and the less you do bad equals a good life. If you do more good and less bad before you die, you will go to heaven or what a good after life after death means for you. A successful life can be solved by a metaphoric math equation. *Do Good Plus Feel Good, Never Do Bad, Never Feel Bad Equals a Good Life.* Quite hard to never feel bad, but make sure you feel good most of the time at least.

Intuition

My biggest failures in life came from not following my intuition Sometimes our intuition is right, but we lack courage, or we have fear. Our intuition is always right. It can often times be a gut feeling that doesn't make much sense. Listening to your intuition is the same as listening to your soul. Your *soul* is always right.

Some of the things that block us from our intuition is bad health, if you are not healthy it is hard to connect your mind, emotions and soul. The alignment of your soul with your personality is a goal that every human should have. When the soul is the one setting the direction, rather than the mind or emotions, then you are definitely taking the right path in life.

Always follow your intuition even if you fear the consequence. A lot of people have deep desires to be something or to dream of having something, but they get held back by logical thought, that it is not possible. They also get held back by the emotions of fear. You can *overcome* obstacles that stop you from listening to your intuition just by writing out what you dreamed to be or have. Your deepest desires are not something that shouts at you and all of the sudden you know it. They usually whisper in your ears, they show up in subtle thought. Next time your intuition tells you to do something, give it a try and take action.

Staying in your Highest Vibrational Frequency

Your Vibrational Frequency can also be simplified as the quality of your thoughts and emotions. The scientific meaning is "*the rate at which atoms and sub-particles of a being or object vibrate. The higher this vibrational frequency is, the closer it is to the frequency of light*". Even in spiritual scriptures of different beliefs they associate love with light.

Love is the highest vibrational frequency, if you consistently put yourself the feeling state of love, you will attract great things. Your vibrational frequency determines what appears in your life. If you have a high vibrational frequency of love, gratitude, joy and bliss, and keep that frequency, you will bring in to your life people and events that give you more of the same. If you have a low vibrational frequency all the time, this is hatred, anger, revenge, guilt, shame, sadness or fear, you will experience these things most of the time. It is a sad reality for those who keep these emotions. These are the emotions to always avoid, these emotions can be removed and replaced from your life.

You can only hold one emotion at a time. Just like in the physical world, if I hold a red basketball in my hand, I cannot put a green one in my hand at the same time. You cannot blend the two basketballs together. So, in your heart you cannot have love and hatred at the same time. You can only feel good at this moment, or bad, you will *never* feel both at the same time. Anytime you are feeling bad, find a way to feel good. The Law of Perpetual Transmutation of Energy states that "*We all have the power within us to change any condition in our lives that we are not happy with. Higher energy vibration will definitely consume and transform the lower ones.*" You have the power to change any negative emotion with positive emotions. Darkness is only the absence of light. Replace any dark emotion by choosing to let light shine with *positive* emotions.

I met a guy who had a broken arm, it was in a sling. He fell off a ladder. He asked me "*What did I do to attract this broken arm in my life*?". I asked him "*How many people do you hate*?". He went on for a few minutes and named about 30 people. I then asked "*Out of these people, did you wish one of them would get in accident, tragedy or die*?". He said "*I don't mind if all of them die, I was hoping some of them did die or get hit by a car or something*."

So, I told him that his wanting and wishing for other people to get hurt caused him to get his arm broken. Anytime you want other people to get hurt, you will be the one in pain. If you hold wishing pain for other The Law of Attraction doesn't know if you want it for another person or yourself. Anytime you're wishing pain or failure for others, you're holding that energy of bad intention. You attracted this pain, because you wished pain on others.

Being able to attract what you want in life is all about changing your vibrational frequency to the thing that you want. The feeling of wealth is the feeling of abundance. This is a high vibrational frequency that allows you to *attract abundance* in your life. Any negative feelings that you feel throughout your day is leading you to have negative experiences. Always consider your vibrational frequency when you go about your day. Are you vibrating at the level of light? It takes work, it takes mental *work* to make changes. Changing how you think is one of the hardest things to do in life. So changing your vibrational frequency is a gradual process also.

Emotional Awareness is one of the key ingredients to change your vibrational frequency. Always pay attention to how your feeling. When you notice you are not feeling good, change how you feel. Choose to *feel love, faith, gratitude* or any good feeling you can.

If you feel really bad or depressed, it might be hard to jump into feeling totally happy all of the sudden. You can climb your way up to feeling good. Choose to feel good and focus on it. Just keep telling yourself "*I feel better*" or "*I feel good*". Smile and repeat to yourself "I *feel good, I feel good, I feel good....*" focus on feeling good and keep smiling. You will notice yourself starting to feel better. Another way to make yourself feel better is meditate yourself to neutral. There is high vibrational frequency, low, and neutral. If you feel bad, you can meditate to neutral and in that meditation start focusing on feeling good, and smile.

For me I made gratitude my neutral point. I do my best to *always feel grateful* all the time, and anytime I feel down, I go straight to feeling grateful. From feeling grateful, I can jump to feeling happy and love easily because they are in the same playing field. It becomes easier for me to be in a good vibrational frequency if I am always feeling a deep sense of gratitude.

Health

It good that the Philippines is starting to be health-conscious. They are starting to workout at the gym more, there is definitely a lot of Zumba going on and yoga is also on the rise. I am glad to see that happening. I hope that this continues and hope the people in the provinces can also start making exercise a part of their daily habit.

It is really important to workout at least 5 times a week; a sure way not to get sick easily and more importantly, stay fit. Join a gym and invest in it. The flaw that I see when it comes to health is Filipinos believe too much in going to the doctor to cure sickness, rather than sickness prevention.

The best way to prevent being sick is exercise *with* diet. I guess I can count as a workout nut, and I hang out with workout nuts. They never get sick, I (*as well*) never get sick. Even when they are sick, they still go on about their day, if it is work or working out. Normal people when they get sick, they stay in bed all day or go to the doctor and ask what what's wrong with them.

The Gym Benefits your Mind, Body and Money

Going to a high-end gym is what going to a golf course used to be. Not only is it good for your health you can make some business connections. The gym that I go to has a lot of business owners and people who are high ranking at big corporations. I've benefited financially and they have also benefited from my services in the exchange, and vice versa. Going to the gym also improves your social skills. There will always be times where people will talk to you for any reason, or you might talk to the trainer and ask how to use a machine. You might run into people that you know, and you end up re-connecting or make new connections and increase your social circle.

The benefits are enormous. You'll become more confidence, your memory will improve, your body will look good, have more energy, and basically never get sick. Let's start with confidence, when you're more confident you can talk to be people with ease, and they'll believe every word you say because you'll be talking with conviction. People will trust a confident person.

Your body alone, you'll look better. A lot of people want to have this dream body that they feel is a perfect body for them. Most people don't have the body they want. The few who has the body they want are usually successful in many areas in their life. When you're able to achieve success in one area with discipline and determination, you can easily achieve success in any other area in life.

It also works the other way around. If you're disciplined at something, like coding, programming, business management, when you start enjoying working out, you'll bring the quality of yourself discipline into it. Eventually you'll start your goal setting for your body and reach it.

Someone once told me the quality of your life depends on the quality of yourself discipline. Even Napoleon hill in the Master Key to Riches no success principle will work without self-discipline. Without sufficient self-discipline success will not be possible.

The Art of Self-Healing

Anyone that really spent time with me knows that I'm not a fan of going to the hospital and defiantly not a fan of getting injected or taking man made pills to try to heal. I noticed that anyone who's under 50 and takes maintenance pills, for whatever reason, is not mentally stable. Those man-made pills effect your mind in negative ways. A lot of people that I know who are dependent on medication to stay not get sick have mental problems. If you're on medication and you're mad about what I just wrote, that might be one of the side effects, easily angered.

One part of healing yourself comes from your mind. Our minds have the ability to heal itself. Our cells are constantly repairing itself and creating new cells. As I said before, what you focus on grows. So usually when someone is sick, they focus on how sick they are. They focus on how bad they feel, they tell people they're sick, so they can get some sympathy.

One of the reasons why I never get sick to the point like I'm bed ridden or unable to work is because I have this method that anyone can use. I used this in seminars and some people instantly feel better. It starts with changing your focus through words and focusing on the feeling of healing. I just repeat to myself “I am healing, I am healing, I am healing....”. I'm thinking I'm healing, I'm feeling I'm healing, therefore I shall be healed.

Most people when they get sick what do they do? They tell everyone they run into that they're sick, they complain to themselves that they're sick. They investigate how they got sick and see if they can blame someone for it. They tell their friend “It's your fault I'm sick! I came home late in your birthday party.” They post on Facebook a selfie with a sad face, and sad emoji, so everyone say's “feel better!”. They repeat “I'm sick, I'm sick, I'm sick.”. But they never repeat “I'm healing, I'm healing, I'm healing.”

This is an example of the power of thought. Your thoughts can make you sick and keep you sick or they can make you healthy and keep you healthy. The great part about it is you're 100% in control of your thoughts. Your thoughts control your body. So, when you focus on yourself being sick then your sickness will remain. When you focus on healing, sometimes you'll instantly feel better. You'll realize that you were carrying the emotion of being sick and you weren't really that sick. Every time you start to get sick, focus and hold on to the feeling of healing.

The physical part of self-healing is don't move. Stay in bed and don't move.

Your Energy System that Processes Your Emotions

The same way we process food, we also process emotions. We have 5 senses, but our sixth sense is our emotions. We release our emotions in two ways. It's either in love and trust, or fear and doubt. As we have a digestive system to process food, we have an energy system that processes our emotions.

Even if you're not aware of your emotions, they are always being produced inside of you. Your energy system never stops functioning so you will always have emotions radiating inside you. No matter what happens in your day, you will have an emotional reaction to many things. If you see a headline in the news that gets you mad, then because of that headline you chose to process your emotion with fear and doubt.

Every emotion has different strengths and characteristics. Anger goes away faster than jealousy. The need for revenge is more persistent than jealousy. This is why in many divorce cases, one party might be very persistent in winning, fueled by revenge. The flow of your emotions will never stop, it will keep going until you physically die.

You have an emotional fingerprint, which means the way you process your emotions is different than anyone else in the world. This is why when you see someone reacting differently than how you would react emotionally, you think "Why do you have to react that way? It's only a phone". Some people cry over a lost phone, some people won't.

When some bad incidents happen to people, some people

might withdraw and become silent, while others might get angry, and others might seek company and conversation with someone. Some people need to be alone, while others need to be around a group of people to process their emotion in a positive way. The best way they know how.

There are two ways we experience life emotionally. It's with fear or love. When you are angry, vengeful, sad, greedy or spiteful, or critical, those are experiences of fear. When you are joyful, grateful, happy, kind and caring. These are experiences of love.

Looking inward, rather than outward is one of the important steps to practice and master spiritual development. Stop looking for external power, the ability to manipulate or control everything and everyone. Rather, focus on having authentic power, the alignment of your personality with your soul.

Rather than seeing the outside world and reacting with emotions. Your goal is not to change your parents, boss, workers, or friends. Your goal is to change yourself. Your most painful emotions show that your resistant to changing. They occur most often because you have failed to make progress. Jealousy, rage, depression, vengefulness might be ruining your life.

Stop trying to explain why circumstances or other people are making you feel bad or sad. Study yourself and know that you are the cause of all of your emotions, even the emotions that torment you. If you break a bone on your arm, it won't stop hurting until you take care of it. Pay attention to what needs to be healed in you first, in order for you to reach true spiritual development.

You can't heal a broken bone by blaming the dumbbell the

stairs you fell from. You can't stop a painful emotion by shouting at people, or shouting at things, or withholding your love. Those things or people are not the cause of your negative emotions. The cause of all of your negative emotions is the way energy is being processed in your energy system.

Try right now, directing your attention towards your energy system, start with your solar plexus, and focus away from anything outside of you. Away from all circumstances and people to blame. Feel whatever you feel now, but start to process the feeling of love and trust. Pay attention to your emotions turning into love and trust. Allow yourself to begin processing all energy inside with love and trust. So that everything you express is love and trust. Practice this, all day, every day, for the rest of your life.

Law of Attraction

I have been studying and teaching the *Law of Attraction* to my workers, friends, people I run into, and grew to doing it for groups and seminars. When I attempt to teach it to people labeled as ignorant, they do not believe in it which now makes them *skeptics*. They think it is some kind of fake magic or satanic thing which is absolutely false. It is a natural law of the universe, just like the *law of gravity.*

When it comes to cause and effect, your thoughts have a cause, and the effect is your actions. Once you take action that also has an effect. If you do not drink water for 10 days you will definitely die of dehydration. Not drinking water is a lack of action, and continuously not doing so will make you die as an effect. It is a scientific fact that you will die from not drinking (adequate amounts of) water.

It is also a fact that you have an energy field that is positive(+) and negative(-). When you think, your whole being vibrates- some may call it your *aura.* If you have a good aura, you will attract good experiences in your life, if it is bad, then you will attract bad experiences.

For those religious people who think The Law of Attraction is Satanic, it is pretty ignorant for them to say that. The Law of Attraction is the mystery that helps your prayers get answered. Your prayers will only be answered if you have faith, a positive emotion, and love the highest frequency emit. If you are passionate about having your prayers answered, they *will be* answered. The level of emotions and faith, and the action you take is the same level of possibility that your prayer will be answered.

If you pray for something, but all throughout the day you complain, have any degree of negative emotion large OR small, and you also are hurtful towards others especially yourself -- your prayer will not be answered. I noticed the biggest complainers live the most miserable lives because they never get what they want, because they complain and see the bad side to everything.

The Law of Attraction works in your favor if you have continuous faith and act in love. The Law of attraction also works against you if you have negative emotions like hatred, rage, doubt, worry, and if you hurt others, you will receive that pain right back in one way or another. Let's get this straight. Everything comes from God and is constantly weighing what you deserve and what you do not deserve. The Law of Attraction tells God, you deserve good things because you are a good person. It is invisible justice. If anyone ever tells you "Life's not fair" let them know they are the one making it unfair, by complaining and taking no action to fix it.

This book contains a lot of useful things I have learned in almost 2 decades. I have been reading books and studying self-improvement for almost 20 years. I decided to put the best of the best in this book. Some of the content might range anywhere from Metaphysical Sciences, Neuroscience and NLP, as well as productivity and business strategies. Since this book's *sole* purpose is to be part of my mission "To Help the Philippines become a First World Nation". I hope every Filipino in the world reads this. It is also a good book to give someone who needs to improve their life.

You're a Magnet that Vibrates and Attracts

Your mind is an attraction-based part the world. It attracts things that correspond to exactly what it thinks and feels. What it thinks and feels it sounds out to the Universe. You are the most important thing in the Universe according to your mind.

This world is also attraction based, we create, or bring towards us everything that has ever happened in our lives. Every event, person, good or bad, you attracted in your life through your thoughts, emotions and actions. This happens all the time with no exceptions. You're the one responsible for all that has ever happened in your life.

When you know how the Law of Attraction works, you can make it work for you. You can have more love, more happiness, better health, more wealth, better people and environmental conditions, and an overall better-quality experience of life. You just have to make some adjustments in your mind, in the way you think, and the things you believe.

How the Law of Attraction Works

Let's consider how the animals in the world began. In the beginning, everything was big. The dinosaurs were all humongous, but they had little thinking abilities. Now compared to the dinosaurs we're small, but we have great thinking abilities. We have thought ability to manifest all we want and need in our lives.

This Universe is energy based. Everything that has ever been created is made of energy. All forms, from water, to rock, to trees, animals and us human beings are made up of different vibrations of energy. Even our thoughts are made of energy.

Everything is made up of the same thing and is connected in matrix of energy. When you ask a Quantum Physicist, they'll tell you "everything is made of the same thing" The whole Universe is made of the same thing.

Things that are liquid, and things that are solid are actually made up of the same thing. They are just vibrating at different rates. So, in reality, we are all one. Just think of yourself as a single cell in the body of the Universe. Everything we think and do effects one another in a subatomic level. We're all energy beings, living in an energy universe. We come from the same thing.

God, or the Universal energy is intelligent and creative and it changes into things straight from its original form. All of this is done starting with thought. Since everything is the same, everything is connected, it has big consequences in the mind and physics the different rates and qualities are frequencies. All vibration is measured by frequency.

Matter is a dense and compact that vibrates at a low frequency and it really doesn't change much or at least not that fast. Water changes more easily and is affected by temperature, it freezes when it's cold and steams when it's hot. Thoughts are so much lighter than water or rocks. They are capable of changing quickly at any moment. With the right amount of thought energy, we can create anything we want in our lives

All energy is Magnetic

Now you know already and understand how you think and feel is magnetic to what you're vibrating. When you become aware of this, you should make it a practice to think positively. Thinking positive is one of the prerequisites to having a successful and happy life. It's really important to keep a handle on how you feel, think and talk. It's also important to stay aware if the people around you are negative or positive.

These aspects affect the life that you live right now. How you think, feel and talk, and the people you hang out with are the ones affecting your life right now and in the future. Everything that you have right now is the result of all of your activity from the past. This is so true for everything going on in your life right now.

Truth about Attraction

Everything in this universe is magnetic Our life conditions are affected by the energy and mix of other people's vibrations and feelings, as we also affect everything and everyone around us with our vibrational frequency. This is all scientific facts.

It's good if we can discipline to think and feel the things we choose. Not the things that show up in front of our face. All that we think about and focus on, we attract to our experience. When we see bad news and focus on it, we will have similar vibrations come to us. So just be more aware of what you're thinking, feeling saying and doing in each moment. Practice awareness and take control of the thoughts you want to think about.

Thoughts Become Things Right?

Thought travels lightly, and it's a very malleable form of energy. Unlike other forms that are visible, thoughts can instantly start the process of creating an experience. An idea is the beginning part of the thought. Our feelings create the experience or things to begin to appear in our lives.

Meaning of Manifestation is to make evident the senses, especially to the sight; to show plainly; to reveal or display what may have at first been obscured or hidden; to appear in visible form. For you to plan a trip with your family, first you have to think about it, you have to decide where you want to go. Then you start researching what hotel to stay at, check your budget and vacation availability and you take the action and manifest that vacation.

Law of Attraction

What we think about and focus on appears in our lives. We manifest it with our intense focus and emotions. When you think of good things most of your day, and you think good things about people, you attract good people and things in your life. You attract the like vibration of what you're thinking.

When someone is focused on crimes, they will most likely end up being the victim of a crime or committing a crime. When you focus on sadness, about how sad people are, or how sad you are, you will manifest more sadness.

It's like in physics, in waves and particles you get more of what you're thinking most of the time, because what you're thinking about is also attracted to you. What you focus on is what is manifested directly into your experience.

So, it's important to think less about the bad things in life, the bad news, bad people, bad incidents that happened in your life, eliminate all negative thoughts. In order to be happy with your life you need to concentrate on all good things. Focus on everything you would like to attract, the opportunities you would like to take on, and good events and people you would like to have in your life.

You need to focus on abundance and harmony in your life. I know that you may be looking for more good things to come in your life and less of the bad things. You might have goals you want to achieve, or maybe you're looking a partner in romance. You have to start focusing on the abundance and opportunities rather than the obstacles

A lot of times it's your negative programming growing up that gets in your way. It's hard to look in the bright side if everyone you grew up with was focused on the lack of life. But later on, I will show how to find what the negative beliefs are that block you and how to eliminate them and replace them with good beliefs.

When you change your beliefs to be more constructive, you will see that everything will fall in place. Good people will appear and all you ever wanted will be in your possession Your life will just get better and better. This is only when you think and feel good and expect good. When you think badly about everything, expect bad things to keep appearing. It's all about how you think. It's time that you begin to change the way you think to attract all good.

Visualization Technique

Every moment that we are awake or even when we're sleeping, we are constantly visualizing something. We're day dreaming, and we're thinking about things. We have very powerful imaginations that can go beyond what we believe is possible.

Every moment we're imagining something. We also notice whatever is happening in the world around us or what we pay attention to and it becomes our reality. As featured in many books from success, law of attraction, sports, or anything that has to do with achieving goals, Visualization is one of the keys to success. How well we visualize is a big factor in how well we manifest.

The first step of visualization is to choose what you want. It's something that basically all of us can do, but for some reason a lot of people are still not clear on what they want. So, understand the first step is to choose. Use your imagination to create what you want to bring in your life. This is actually a natural process that we do every day. The problem is most people are subconsciously choosing what they want.

Use your mind to think and make pictures of what you want. If I ask you to visualize what your bed looks like, I'm pretty sure you can easily see what it looks like without really having to use much effort. Sometimes you might not be able to visualize it clearly because your visualization muscle isn't strong enough yet. This is a muscle that can be improved upon.

Creative Visualization

Without even knowing, most of us are doing creative visualization every day. We do it when we're asleep and when we're awake. We visualize what we have to do, like buy groceries, change clothes, take a shower or any other thing, we need to do, before we do it. It's time you use visualization to design the life you want. Like how an architect visualizes a castle, before building it.

We all have different ways to visualize. Some people see a movie, some see pictures, some really can't visualize anything but the just imagine the feeling can still manifest things they want. We all have different ways of dealing with our own thoughts.

When you want the outcome, you desire in your life, you have to take control of your imagination. What you imagine consistently and focus on, you bring into your life. When your mind is continuously wandering and ends up thinking about good things, then bad things, then good things, it won't manifest what you really want, because it's not focused thinking. Keep your attention and focus on what you want.

The more intense your focus the stronger you visualize. There are different levels of strengths when it comes to creative visualizing. Some people can visualize in every detail, from color, shapes, even smell. It's important to put strong feelings as well, sometimes even if you can't visualize it clearly, as long as your feeling is strong, it will still manifest. But if you have a really clear vision of what you want, and you have intense desire for its achievement you will manifest much faster.

Your Visualization has to be Positive

In Silva Mind Control where they put you in an alpha state, or in meditation where you are at peace, this is the best state you can be in when you visualize. When your body is at rest, because when your body has no tension it means there's no negative emotions. Stay aware of your attitude also when you visualize, make sure it's positive, and your feelings, make sure it's happy and filled with love.

When you feel angry about something and you hold on to it while you visualize it won't do you any good. When you're in a negative state you're blocking yourself from any good. Remember when you are negative you push the things you want away from you. Take your time to make yourself feel good before visualizing anything.

When things are going good it's so much easier to visualize more good things. So, if your life is doing pretty good right now then keep bringing it to higher levels with positive visualization. If it's not doing good, being able to visualize the good things might be difficult, but it's the best way to get out of the conditions that might not make you happy. When you keep your feeling of happiness and have clarity in your visualizations more opportunities, good people and good events will come into your life.

In NLP they use a way to get in a positive state of mind. You can use it too. Just sit somewhere comfortably, close your eyes, and relax every part of your body.

Wealth

Let's talk about money now. It's time that the Philippines becomes or at least aim to become a first world nation. There should one day come a time where every day there's a thousand new Filipino millionaires. I feel this time will come soon.

It's not just for Filipino's but a lot of people all over the world. The average person thinks that everything just happens to them. Like their life is just based on luck and chance. Well this really isn't the case. You create your own life. You're 100% responsible for everything that happens to you today onward

Aiming to survive is also something that stops people from getting rich. If you aim hoping not to lose money or just to make enough money to pay your debt or buy food, then you won't get rich. You have to set higher standards and aim to be rich.

Thinking too small is one thing that I see often. People want to go in business to make one peso at a time. They want to make money from a "peso" a lot of times it can end up in big profits, many times it's just an additional income. Think about it this way. The same energy you think of planning or managing your "peso peso" empire, is the same energy you could be using to plan and manage a "Million Million" empire.

Focusing on problems is also another problem. People who focus on problems always have a lot of problems, and worse, if there's no problem they'll look for a problem. It's better not to focus on your problems and just focus on your opportunities and solutions.

Hating rich people is a big obstacle that I went through also. I grew up being somewhat jealous of rich kids, I think it's normal. Now that we know this way of thinking isn't good it's time, we don't think this way anymore. Imagine, if you want to be rich, why would you criticize rich people? You should start making a list of rich people you admire.

If you have friends that are not successful, or pull you down every time you want to get back up, you need to get rid of them if you want to get rich. Successful people associate themselves with other successful people. While the unsuccessful people associate with unsuccessful people. If you don't know any successful people, join some groups that might have successful people and meet them.

A hindrance that I see all too often is people with skills and abilities, but they don't know how to promote themselves. Don't look at selling as something bad, don't look at self-promotion as something bad. You should spread the word out about how good you are at your craft and get people to pay you for your services.

You can tell the size of a person by the size of their problem. Some people get stressed out or are unable to solve small problems. Don't let your problems be bigger than you. You should always be bigger than your problem. Problem solving is a skill, and any skill can be improved. Successful people and unsuccessful people have problems every day. It's just the quality of the problems differ.

I've also seen a lot of unsuccessful people reject good things. They don't take compliments well, they don't take money, unless you force them to take it. They're just not good at receiving because they feel they don't deserve good things. You should make yourself an excellent receiver and when someone complements you or gives you money, receive it, smile, and say thank you.

Workers mentality is also something that stops people from getting rich. They just want to get paid by the hour. Getting paid by the hour puts a ceiling in your income. The best type of jobs that get people rich are jobs that get you paid by results. It can be project based jobs, or sales results. Find ways to make money that's results based.

Many people think it's "either this or that". Thinking that if you spend your time building a business, you won't have enough time with your family. Limited thinking and scarcity mentality cause people to believe that if they have money, they won't have time for fun. Just keep in mind that you can have both. You can have success financially, personally and be healthy also.

Eventually you should also be able to track your net worth. Most people just measure their wealth from how much money they're making each week or month. This is OK, but true wealth is knowing your net worth. This includes your house or any property you own, how much your business is worth,

Money management and financial planning is also something that Filipino's need to learn and master. No matter how much money you make, if you mismanage your money, you won't be able to build wealth. Money management will help you build wealth. If you have a bad habit of spending your money then you have to get rid of this habit and start learning to manage and save money. Until you show you can handle your money, you won't get more.

Are you working hard for money or is money working hard for you? A lot of people work hard for money and this is good. It can be good for a part of your life to work hard for money, but eventually you have to let money work hard for you. Warren Buffet said if you're not making while you're sleeping, you'll be working for the rest of your life. If you want to retire young and be financially secure for your old age, find ways to make money while you're sleeping.

A lot of people are unsuccessful or haven't reached their dreams because they allow fear to stop them. There are so many ideas in the world that haven't been manifested because of fear. The easiest way to get rid of fear is to take action. Even if you have fears, take action anyway. You'll see that it's just "False Evidence Appearing Real" and realized trying to make your ideas come alive is actually good.

Unsuccessful people think they know everything, and aren't willing to learn anything new. Successful people are always looking for something new to learn, something they can use for their business, happiness or health. Once you start learning new things each day to improve on your skills, you will be irreplaceable

It's time now that you start learning and growing. This section is something for you to know what obstacles you might have mentally that you need to correct in order for you to get rich. I will now declare that every Filipino in the world who reads this book, now has an obligation and life purpose to get rich, and allow their wealth to help the country.

Importance of Clarity

It's very important for you to have clarity in what you want. The clearer you are about what you want, the more confidence you have that you'll achieve it resulting to more action taken towards what you want to achieve. The clearer the vision the better the results.

When you have only a vague picture of what you want to achieve it's not powerful. Concentrated attention to a clear picture brings the best results, it brings the thing you want coming towards you. So, you really should be spending a lot of time in being clear in what you want in life.

Some Top of the Line Visualization tips

The first step to take before visualization is to relax. Put yourself in a meditative state, in a state of trance, get your brain frequencies into alpha level. It's important to have a positive state of calmness, peace, harmony and abundance inside. Seeing the world in a calm and harmonious state and feeling abundance is great for manifesting what you want. Acknowledge what you already have in your life and give thanks for all of it and feel abundant already.

When you feel abundance, it's so much easier to attract abundance. It's faster and easier to energize from a feeling and being abundant. Any state you're in creates more of the same. So, when you have mind of abundance, more abundance cells will grow in you before you even visualize what you want, it's important to have a high vibrational state of abundance before you begin to create clarity of what you want in your mind.

In order for you to feel abundance start by noticing how grateful you are of all the good things in your life already. We all have something to be grateful for. It might be your health, your family, your ability to see and hear, your children, your partner, your parents, your job, your business, the food you're eating, your ability to do things that others can't do. You could be thankful for all the kind people that ever entered your life, for all the kindness that anyone has ever given to you. The knowledge you've learned and thankful for the people who gave you that knowledge. Everyone should have a big list to be thankful for.

If you think your list is small and you don't have much to be grateful for, start appreciating the fresh air you're breathing, the eyes you have to read this book. Be thankful for the last time you received money no matter how small the amount. Be thankful for anyone that loves you and is kind to you. Be thankful you're able to eat every day, and be thankful you're alive.

After you're in a calm state of gratitude and abundance Begin to visualize the thing that you want. On another level you can begin to visualize your perfect day. After you have achieved all your goals, what would your perfect day look like?

Questions to help Visualize your Perfect Day
Start from when you wake up in the morning.

1. Where are you?
2. What do you see when you wake up?
3. Who's with you? Are you with someone you love?
4. Who are you with in the place you live?
5. What's your morning routine?
6. Are you exercising? What's your exercises routine?
7. What does your bathroom look like? Is it big? Are you taking a bath or shower?
8. What type of soap and shampoo are you using? Is it luxurious?
9. When you're getting ready to put on clothes, what does your closet look like?

10. What kind of clothes are you getting ready to put on?
11. What activities are you doing in the morning? Are you reading? Swimming?
12. What are you having for breakfast?
13. Did you make breakfast? Or do you have maids that prepare your food?
14. While you're eating breakfast are you with people you love?
15. Do you have pets?
16. Are you preparing to go to work or a business you own?
17. Do you love the work you do?
18. Are you working at home?
19. Do you not have to work anymore because you have assets working for you?
20. What kind of business and investments do you have?
21. Are you going to a meeting with Billionaires today?
22. Are you a Millionaire or Billionaire?
23. Are you living an abundant life with more than enough money for generations after you?
24. During the day are you helping people?
25. Are you involved or donating in a charity?
26. Are you someone that makes the world a better place?
27. Are you spending the day with your family and people you love?
28. Are you going on vacation with people you love?
29. Where do you go when you go on vacation?
30. If someone asks you where you traveled, what would you say? How would you say it?
31. What's your level of happiness this perfect day?
32. What's your level of energy and love for life?
33. What is your health and nutrition like?
34. What restaurants do you like to eat these days?
35. Where do you go shopping?
36. What kind of jewelry or clothes do you own?

37. What success symbols do you have?
38. Are you driving a luxury car? Or are you being driven?
39. Are you driving fast in a Ferrari?
40. Do you own a boat?
41. Are you taking private jets to different places all over the world?
42. Is your perfect day more like being in the woods?
43. What is your perfect day?
44. How does the day end for you?
45. Are you eating dinner in your house?
46. Are you in a restaurant?
47. Are you doing some kind of work like presenting on stage during night time?
48. Are you famous and people want to take a picture with you while eating dinner?
49. Are you watching a movie in your private cinema in your house?
50. Are you taking a helicopter from your office to your mansion?

So, these are some questions that might help stimulate some details of what you want to visualize in your life. Some people they visualize the perfect day that is about 5 to 10 years away. Once you do this you have a long-term view of what you want and your subconscious mind will start going towards it. Get clarity in your perfect day before you have clarity in your short-term goals. Sometimes we visualize some short-term goals, but it might lead us away from our perfect day.

Not Just seeing, visualize an Experience

While in a harmonious state of abundance, start to

experience what you want in life. Feel and know that you have it already, create your feelings as being the person who has what they want. Experience being the person you want to be, experiencing what you want. Visualize yourself being successful, being praised, being in business, being wealthy, being healthy, being happy, being the cause of change. Visualize yourself being that person already.

Imagine the attitude of the person you want to be. Sometimes our attitude is the biggest difference. Are you successful? Do you have control of your emotions? Are you emotionally capable of handling big challenges that affect a lot of people? Is your attitude kind to other people? Do you have high standards for yourself? Do you have higher work ethics? Are you learning every day? Are you doing everything in excellence? Are you giving your best effort at everything you do?

When you begin to clearly experience the state of mind and attitude of the person you want to be, you have more clarity in how you will get tangible things. In order to get tangible things in life you have be someone different than who you are right now. Any change outside your body starts with a change inside your mind. When you start being in alignment with the state of mind and attitude of someone who has the things you want to manifest the law of attraction starts reacting to the vibrational frequency you emit at this moment.

This is a magnetic universe and when your vibrations start to transmit being the person who already has the things that you want the universe will bring the things you want into your life. Once you continuously experience being the version of you that has already has everything they want, you will soon experience things showing up in your life as they are supposed to.

Anyone Can Get Rich

If enough Filipino's have a success mindset then the whole country's economy will become better. We'll be smart enough, and work together for a common goal to help the country become a first world nation. Even if the effects won't arrive until generations after us, at least we can get the momentum going for generations to come. We all have an obligation to make the country better for the next generation.

Even if you want to be successful for yourself and for people you love, it is really difficult to live a good life if you're always in debt and having a hard time surviving. You won't be able to maximize the expression of your talent and passions without enough money. You won't be able to develop your physical or spiritual powers without enough money. You won't be able to enjoy things like car's, gadgets, travel, or have the lifestyle you deserve without enough money.

One of the goals in life is to develop to our full potential so it's your duty be rich. You shouldn't settle for less or be satisfied with whatever you've been able to earn so far, if you're truly not happy with the amount you're making. God put you on this earth to be Kings and Queens of I kingdom, how big or small you wish to have it. To be content with less than you deserve is a sin.

If you have all you want in life, you're rich. Every person naturally want's the be the most they are capable of being. It's our natural desire to want more. We can only be more by making use of what we have, and what we're able to give.

I know most people have been thought that wanting money

is evil. This is one of the biggest beliefs that hold people back from getting rich. It's OK to want money. Avoid being a person who don't desire to live in abundance to have all they want in life. You're desire to live abundant is beneficial for all the people you love and more.

Sure, we all have different values in life. Some people value family, friends, spirituality, food, exercise, or fun experiences. In order to enjoy all of these things we need money to buy food, we need money for transportation to meet friends, we need money to buy clothes for our family, even in spirituality you need money to tithe.

Most children and teenagers desire to be rich and believe in themselves that they can be rich when they become adults. When they become adults, they lose that desire. It's time to bring that desire back, because now when you keep reading, you'll have a strategy to be rich. To be of service means being the most you can be, the more money you have, the more people you can help.

My Observation of People who became Rich

Have you ever noticed that not every rich man's son or daughter become rich? A lot of them just make enough to get by. Plenty of them have squandered their parent's fortune. Most people who were raised poor, stay poor, or become a little bit more successful financially than their parents. A lot of super rich people started out poor or lower middle class. Middle class and rich people, same thing.

Getting rich and becoming wealthy isn't about luck or anything close to that. It's an algebra equation, I'll show you the equation so you can solve the problem and become rich. The result of having riches depends on your success attitude. No matter how hard you work if you don't have an attitude of success you won't get rich.

When it comes to accumulating wealth and being rich it doesn't matter where you were born. Yet it does matter a bit, but I'm sure you met many people who came from the other side of the world. It also doesn't matter what City or Town you live in. In every town there's rich, poor and middle class. Two people might be in the same business, one fails another succeeds. The other succeeded because of success mentality.

I also noticed that many rich people don't really have or need talent, they don't need to look good, they're a lot of rich people who are fat, who are short, some of them are not even smart. There's a lot of rich people who have only average intelligence and they became rich. You're better than many rich people one way or another.

What part of town you're born can't stop you? There's internet now, sometimes you don't even have to leave your house and you can make money. If you want to do a brick and motor business you can do well in your town or in a City where more people are and make more money. Part of getting rich includes dealing with people, the money always has to come from someone. So, you might have to connect online or wherever you live.

Just because you live in the Philippines, don't think you can't be rich. There are so many people who are Billionaires, and thousands of Millionaires in Dollar value, born and raised in the Philippines, many of them didn't have to leave the country. They just made use of their talents and passions that best suits them. You can be the poorest person in your town, but if you have a successful attitude and can imagine yourself being rich while taking action towards your goals, you'll end up as the richest person in your town.

Endless Opportunities

Opportunity has dramatically increased compared to 30 years ago. All because of the internet and the growing demand of skilled workers. Don't think that just because you're in the Philippines you're limited to opportunities. All you really have to do is increase your skills. The more skills you have, the more opportunities you have. The higher-level skills you have, meaning the more difficult it is to replace you, the more income you can make.

It's time for us to get rid of the belief that we have lack of opportunities because of the government, or because that's just how it is around here. I see so many people hiring every day, sometimes companies hire by the hundreds or thousands. Even the BPO industry now takes high school graduates, when before you needed to be a college graduate. So, there's more opportunities now than ever.

Even people who are working minimum wage, they have many ways to create extra income and save money. Anyone working in a minimum wage job can also increase their skills in their spare time, rather than hanging out with friends, or spending their free time on social media and YouTube They can save up for a computer and learn skills anywhere from graphic design, writing, sales, marketing, software development, programming, coding, anything they feel passionate about. They can also use their free time enrolling in classes or self-studying to improve. Once they have enough skills, they can easily make more money on their own, or get a higher paying job.

We shouldn't think that our opportunities are kept from us by people. Everything comes from God and enters our lives through the Law of Attraction. When we start believing that people are keeping opportunity from us, our focus goes on lack of opportunity, and we become unable to see opportunity even if it's in front of our face.

This world is abundant in resources and money. There's enough money in the world, if spread evenly to make everyone in the world a Millionaire. The bad side of this is if we spread the money evenly, most people wouldn't be able to keep it because they don't have the success mentality enough to see themselves as millionaire's so they'll end up spending it and going back to the same amount of money they're comfortable with. They'll go back to struggle.

Keep in mind opportunity comes from God, not from other people. We can only see opportunity if we look for it and focus on it. We also have to prepare for opportunity by increasing our skills and abilities. The more value we can give to the world with our skills, the more opportunities we have.

Ultimate Success

One of the bad parts about people in general is they think that someone is supposed to give them a good life. They think it's the luck of the draw. The other bad part is they blame other people if their life isn't doing so well. But the truth is the only person responsible for giving you a good life is you.

If you want success have to take 100% responsibility for

everything that happens in your life. You're responsible for how much money you make, your relationships, your health and fitness, what kind of car you drive, what kind of house you live in, and your future.

The first part is give up blaming people, and the second part is give up all your excuses. Most people who are failures are the ones who have the habit of making excuses all the time. If you ask someone why didn't they reach certain goals, they'll blame someone else or they'll tell you an excuse. For example, if I ask Bob "Why aren't you a Millionaire already?" he'll say "Because the market's down, I haven't really had time to work on my goals, my boss isn't paying me as much as I deserve. I'll just wait, maybe one day I'll be a millionaire."

Truthfully life doesn't care about your excuses. The world doesn't care about who you're blaming. If you're not getting the results you want, that's all your fault. For now, quit blaming other people and make changes. You might have to make changes in your strategy if it's not working and the amount of action, you're taking to reach your goals. Stop wasting your time and energy on blame, because that same energy can be used for progress.

Responsibility for your Emotions

Another thing that you should take responsibility for is how you feel every moment of the day. If you blame other people for making you feel bad, then you're just helpless You're not taking 100% responsibility of your life if you wait for other people to make you feel good. If someone intentionally tries to hurt your emotions. You might get hurt at the moment, but it's your choice if you want to dwell on that emotion or let go of that emotion.

There will always be pain, and time heals all wounds, but there's ways to heal faster. One way is choose not to react to negative people or situations. You can do See no evil, hear no evil, speak no evil method. Choose not to pay attention to whatever just happened, or whatever negative thing was said to you. Choose your reaction or don't react at all and focus on something you love. Like I say the only thing in your mind and your heart should be love and goals. If it's not related to love and goals then you don't have to think about it.

There are so many examples of people in extreme situations like prisoners of war, people who were tortured by Nazi's and people who went through tragedies. Some of these people were able to control their emotions and imaginations. Some prisoners of war were able to just imagine themselves playing golf or imagine they were eating a three-course meal. They were able to control their emotions even in a prison cell. If you're reading this you most likely have freedom. It should be easy for you to control your emotions.

Stop Complaining

One of the reasons why people are negative is because they always focus on something to complain about. For you to complain you believe that something better exists. If you're complaining about your car, you know there's a better car out there. If you're complaining about your job, you know there's a better job. When you complain you're reacting the wrong way. If you notice yourself complaining about something you have power to change, then instead of complaining, start making some changes. The energy you're using to complain, is the same energy you could use to make changes.

When you do complain, make sure it's to the right person. I've been bothered at restaurants when these loud call center people complain about work. Nothing against call center people, just some of them get loud in restaurants and it's mostly complaining. It's understandable since a lot of them are taking complaint calls. They complain to the co-workers if there's something that needs to be fixed in the system, instead of complaining to people who can make the changes. So, if you do complain, don't complain to someone who can't do anything about it.

You are the Creator of Your Life

Anything that you think say and do has an effect in your life. You're the direct cause of everything that ever happened in your life this includes all of your actions and inaction in every moment you create what happens to you in the future. The actions you take or don't take will affect your life. If you wake up one day broke, in debt, and no one really cares about you. You created that.

The good part of being the creator of your life, is you can make it the way you want it. If you can be, do and have anything you want in life. If you want to be wealthy, you can be wealthy. The thing is you just have to make the right decisions, have the right attitude, and be aligned with what you want to create in your life.

Some steps you can start taking is make a list of what's not working in your life. List down everything that you're not satisfied with. What are the goals you want to achieve but you're not achieving them? If you're in debt list down you have some money problems. If you're relationships aren't working list that down. If you hate your job list that down.

You have to go face to face with your problems. Don't hide your problems with excuses. Face your problems, know what they are, so you can start creating solutions for them.

Once you list your problems down, write down all the solutions you can think of to solve them. Also write down what's working in your life. If your life is going great then keep doing more of that. The goal is to get rid of everything that's not working in your life and do more of what's working in your life. Whatever is working and making you happy and good for you, then keep doing that. Pay attention to your results. If you keep getting the results you don't want, then get rid of what's not working. If you keep getting the results you want, then you're doing the right thing.

Stop Bragging about Being a Victim

"Oh, my life is horrible because I grew up in a broken family". A lot of people grew up in broken families and ended up happy, healthy and wealthy. Some people grew up with no parents, some people have learning disabilities, some people have no arms. All of us are born with advantages and disadvantages in life. If you focus on your disadvantages and talk about it, and make it an excuse for being unhappy or not being able to reach a goal. It means you need to stop playing the victim role.

We're all victims of something. If you choose to hold on to it, focus on it, and tell everyone about your victim story then you will remain a helpless victim to your story. But if you choose to never talk about it, forget about it, focus on what's working and what you're doing right, then you will see good results. The only time you should talk about your victim story, is if you overcame it, found a solution, and inspire others to triumph over this victim story that others might need a solution for.

Have Clarity of Your Future

Know what your major purpose in life is and learn what you have to learn, plan what you have to plan and schedule your time and effort so you can achieve your major purpose. All of us are born with a major purpose. It's important for you to know your major purpose be passionate on achieving it.

My Purpose is to help the Economy of the Philippines my businesses, Self-Improvement and Business Training, and Charity for kids who can't afford to go school. I believe in this and I'm enthusiastic about seeing eventual results. Even if I know there's a big chance I won't see the Philippines become a First World Nation in my lifetime, I know that if I start the trend and change the way Filipino's think, have businesses that provide jobs, and create more educated Filipino's, then seeing these results will be worth my effort.

A lot of people may look at my goals as something grand and out of this world or even impossible. Your life purpose doesn't have to be as big as mine. Some people just want to have a good family life, be a good mom or dad, and raise good kids. Their life purpose might be based on having a perfect family. This can be good, but I've seen a lot of women who have this purpose, fulfill the purpose and when their kids become

All of us should have a purpose we can say in one sentence. Here' some life purpose statements that people have to give you an idea.

- To always improve my life and the lives of others
- To be one of the richest person's in the world
- To make the world a better place
- To eliminate poverty
- To help as many people as I can be the healthiest, they ever been
- To be the best teacher I can and make long term positive impact in all my students

Some people might call it a life purpose, and some may call it an Ikigai. This is a Japanese word that means "The reason you jump out of bed every morning". When you wake up, are you sluggish and would rather continue sleeping rather than start your day? Or are you excited for the new day so you can continue following your Ikigai? It's a beautiful thing when a person finds a purpose in life and is enthusiastic every day on making progress.

Sometimes your Ikigai doesn't have to be progress. It can also be to spend time with people you love. Some grandparents or great grandparents, they might not be working anymore, some have no passion for making financial progress. Their Ikigai can be as simple as spending time with grandchildren. There's a lot of old people don't have this privilege, and those who do cherish it. This is a beautiful thing. As a working adult, I spend a lot of time working. So, when I get old, it would be nice to be excited every morning to spend time with my grandchildren and great grandchildren possibly.

Dig deep and find out why you're doing things. You might taking up engineering because your dad is an engineer and he told you to take it. But deep inside you want to do something more creative, like web design or graphic arts.

If the reason you're doing something doesn't come from you, then you need to think twice if the ladder's facing the wrong wall. I seen people get two college degrees because the first one was because someone else wanted them take it, and the second was because they want it.

You might have heard this before, but now it's time to take action on it. Figure out what you really love to do and organize your life to find a way to make a living out of it. Even if what you love to do is something weird, there has to be a way to make a living out of it. The earlier you can figure this out the better. Start brainstorming and make a list of things you love to do. To be sure about the finances, pick the one that seems like it can make the most money. To be sure about happiness, choose the one that brings you the most joy.

Know What You Want in Life

What's the point of taking action if you don't know what you want? You'll just be running around like the Tasmanian Devil, it will be destruction and chaos. Before taking any major steps, make sure you know exactly what you want. Most people never get what they want, because they really don't know what they want.

As a child most of us were pretty optimistic about the future. We thought we would be driving the most expensive cars, living the same type of life as people in the movies. We thought we'd travel the world. Although I'm sure some of the things we day dreamed about came to a realization. There's still a lot of missing pieces for most people. A lot of major things about how our life would be changed as we get scolded by our parents, teachers and people of authority. After getting in trouble we also become afraid to express what we truly want when it comes to career. All these authority figures and even peers will tell you what career you should begin. So, most people end up starting off on the wrong wall.

Never Settle for Less

You can achieve anything you want in this world. Not being clear on what you want automatically makes you less than what you're capable of. Don't settle for average when you know you can be great. Try to ask yourself what is it that you really want? Or if you're too focused on what you don't want in life, ask yourself what you do want? One dangerous thing in life isn't aiming high and missing it. It's aiming low and reaching it.

In order for you to start having clarification on what you want you can start listing all the things that you love to do and all the things that you want. List 30 things you love to do, and 30 things that you want. This should give you some clarification on the things you want. Some people like art, writing, music, accounting, business, talking to people. Everyone wants different things in life, so don't think there's not enough for you to get what you want.

Your future is what you create by accident or on purpose. The clearer you are about your future; more natural it will be to create it. For you to get where you want to be, you should have a vision of what you want. Make it clear what you want. If it's to be a movie star, popular singer, to have a good work life balance, to be in business, to travel and get paid for it. When you know what you want everything will just flow naturally.

Once you know what you want, you should have a plan on how to get it. Although sometimes a plan doesn't come into your mind right away. A plan can begin from little ideas here and there, flash insights are important to take note of especially when you don't have a plan yet. Eventually you should have a plan, make it as detailed as you feel will be effective for you. Make sure you're doing something every day and it's on course with your plan. If your plan fails, make another plan, and another plan, and keep going until you make a plan that succeeds.

Stay Quiet and Let Your Success Roar

To show your vision to others can also distort it. When you tell people about your vision, they will talk back with opinions, and what to change, and what they think is possible. By the end of the conversation you won't be so sure about your vision. Especially if your vision is grand, you shouldn't be telling anyone about it. The last time I told someone about my vision they thought I was crazy.

Everyone you know only knows a small part of you. Most people want to think they're better than you. Have you ever noticed? Everyone thinks they're better than everyone else. So, when you tell them a vision you have of yourself in the future, they'll start to feel small and put you down for it. They'll look for loopholes and flaws.

They don't want to see you doing better than them. Especially never tell your vision to someone who doesn't even have a vision. What positive outcome would you expect when you talk about your vision to someone who's lost? Keep it to yourself. It's also possible, just like goals, if you talk about your vision, you won't do anything to pursue it, because after spending your energy talking about it, you'll feel like you did something about it, then end up doing nothing.

If you tell someone you have an idea or a plan, most people will just talk to you about it or change the subject. The only time when you can share your Vision is when you're already doing something about it. When you're making progress on your vision and you share it with a good friend who's always uplifting or someone that might be able to help you with your vision. You'll start to notice how doors open. If you have a vision of making an animal shelter to help stray animals and you already have a few animals at your house and you have limited resources, someone you talk to might give you funding or offer a vacant property to help you.

Anything is Possible Mentality

If you don't believe in yourself, no one else will. One of the reasons people never make it to where they want to be in life is, they don't believe in themselves. Understand that the law of life is belief, whatever you believe becomes your reality. If you don't believe you can achieve what you want, then you're sabotaging your own success. You don't even have to worry about other people trying to stop you. If you don't believe in yourself, no one has to try to stop you. They'll just watch you fail.

You got to start believing that nothing is impossible. You can achieve anything you want in life. There's a lot of medical experiments done about the placebo effect or even imaginary surgery Where the patients healed taking medicine that had no effects, and recovered from injuries from telling the patient they did surgery and they'll be back to normal.

You can achieve anything you want in life as long as you put you put your mind to it. Like Henry Ford said "If you think you can, or think you can't. Either way you're right" Or Napoleon Hill "Whatever the mind can conceive and believe, it can achieve." Even in religions they always mention that nothing is possible without faith. For you to achieve what your vision in life you have to believe in yourself. Believe with every fiber of your being that you can achieve what you want.

Confidence in yourself is important. Without confidence you won't achieve much. The level of your confidence is always congruent to the level of your achievements. Know deep inside that you have what it takes to achieve your goals, and if you really don't have what it takes right now, you're making yourself better so eventually you'll have what it takes. Confidence is essential in any achievement.

It's a state of mind or attitude when you have confidence. A lot of us, including me, didn't grow up confident, but I learned how to be confident and worked on it. The amount of actions you take towards a goal or winning at something, depends on the amount of confidence you have. If you have lack of confidence, you'll take lackful action, if you have a lot of confidence, you'll take a lot of action. Confidence an attitude that you can use right now.

One of the reasons why we don't believe in ourselves is we limit ourselves of thinking what we can't do. The phrase "I can't" is something that you should never say. This is a dis-empowering phrase. It's a poisonous phrase. Never talk about what you can't do or any limitations you have. When you start saying "I can't quit smoking, I can't get the job I want, I can't find my soulmate." You stop yourself from even trying.

Some people go through their whole lifetime even believing they can't do something. If they turned back time and carried an attitude of confidence and self-belief, they'd realize that they really can achieve what they want if they have self-belief. In this case you still have a chance, it's still possible for you to have all that you want in life. Get rid of "I can't" today.

It's never too late to make major changes in your life. I know some people who became teachers at 60 years old. While most people that age believe it's not possible, this woman believed, went for it, and now she has a nice career as a teacher.

Some people waste years at a career they hate simply because they never believed they can achieve what they want. Never say "I'm too old" because there's a lot of people who became successful after the age of 40, 50 or 60. Some of them were in the wrong profession for years until they found out what they loved to do, believed in themselves, and went for it.

Never believe your too young also. You don't need to be old to write a novel, you can write a novel. There are best-selling novels written by teenagers. You can start a business at any age, you can make your own tech company at the age of 13 like some kids have done. Especially if you have kids, never tell them they're too young to go for their goals.

When it comes to education, never believe you need a college degree to be successful. I made this mistake, I went to college a few months and stopped going because I wasn't going anywhere. I always believed since I was a child that you don't need a college degree to create a business. For some professions you need a college degree, and there's no way around that, unless you can get someone to pull some strings.

What you do need is specialized knowledge and continuous learning when it comes to developing yourself. This is important to achieve high levels of success. Self-learning is something that will also change your beliefs in a good way. You can learn many ways to improve your self-confidence, your belief system, and strategies to reach your goals just by researching, buying books and going to seminars.

The Importance of Goal Setting

Sometimes happiness comes from setting goals that give us energy, brings our hopes up and helps other people. After knowing your life purpose, and having a vision, you need to have a plan to achieve them. This should be a set of goals that you need to achieve. Some can be in the later future; some can be in the near future. In the section we'll set some long term and short-term goals that you can take action on daily and be sure to track and measure your progress.

Any goal that we put in our subconscious mind we will go after all day every day. If we don't put goals in our mind, we'll just go in circles. If you set clear goals, you'll earn 10, 20 or 100 times more than what you're earning right now. If you write down your goals, I step closer to achieving them then just thinking about them. If you measure your progress weekly, you have a definite chance of achieving your goals.

Specific Goal

Let's go for a number goal. How much money would you like to have in your bank account? When is the deadline in having this money? Your goal should be as clear as possible, the clearer you are about your goal the better the results. When your goals are wishy washy, you'll have bad results. Be specific on what you want.

You can say "I want $1,000,000.00 in my dollar account 5 years from now" or I want "P10,000,000.00 in my BDO Bank account January 13, 2018, 1:30PM." It should be specific and in detail. If you want to live in a Mansion a year from now then write it out in detail, the place, how it looks, everything.

A lot of people can plan the weekend, or they can plan a vacation, but they don't take time to put in clarity what they want financially. When you write the amount of money you want, write also what your life will be like. Will it change? Will you have a nicer house, or car? Will you let your kids go to the best schools? Travel the world? Prepare to grow in order to achieve your goals. If you already had what it takes to reach your goals, you would have achieved it already. So, you need to grow in knowledge and action.

What's Your Major Goals?

You can also have what I call Major Goals, which are goals that if you achieved them, your life will dramatically change. All the other things you want in life will be yours. Everything will seem to work in your favor. These goals include, writing a book, losing 40 pounds, being the president of your company, opening your business, being in a magazine, or filming your movie.

These goals should be under your control. You should be able to measure your progress weekly, quarterly and daily. You should schedule time to make progress in your goals daily. It should be part of your daily routine. If it's not scheduled, and you're not taking action daily, it's only a dream. If you're taking half steps, like you take action one day, then stop for 5 days, then take a bit of action again. There's something wrong with your confidence. There may also be something wrong with your desire. Daily action shows you have the desire to reach your goals, and you have the confidence it will turn out the way you visualized it.

Can you imagine how beautiful it feels to have a major goal and take passionate effort in attaining it? Let's say you set a goal that you know, if you achieved it, it would change your life big time. All you had to do was increase your enthusiasm, confidence and grow your skills as you're going for the win. Wouldn't you stop wasting your time on other things and chase your goal? Write down your major goal that would change your life right now.

Constant Reminders of Goals

Every day you should be looking at your goals at least 5 times a day. There's a lot of ways you can do this. So, choose the best one for you. One is you can rewrite your goals 5 times a day and after writing visualize your goals being achieved. If you're not good at visualizing write down your goals with a vision map of your achievements. This is a whole brain exercise and I've seen it work like magic.

Let's say you have 5 major goals for the next 3 months. One goal might be your body goal, one is financial, another is relationship, project goal, and skill goal. Write down your 5 major goals, read them out loud once, and then look at your vision map. Then close your eyes and imagine the vision map in your head. You can take it a step further also and experience in detail the achievement of your goals.

Always reminding yourself of your goals will help you increase your desire to achieve them. You'll also come up with insights and ideas on how to be more effective in achieving them. Another way to remind yourself of your goals is to write it in an index card and keep with you at all times. The first thing in the morning and last thing at night you can read your goals out loud and imagine how your life would be when you achieved them. Your goals will sink into your subconscious mind.

Your Major Goal, or your Greatest Goal, should be kept in your wallet at all times. You can write this in an index card, but if it's a money goal, you can write a check out to yourself for the amount of money you want to have. Depends on the person, sometimes the index card works better for others, and sometimes a check works better. Why not try both? Keep these reminders in your wallet and review them throughout the day.

Unlimited Achievement

Don't limit yourself to a few goals when you really can achieve anything you want in life. Think about it, in 25 to 50 years you can achieve monumental success. Sure, you might haven't see someone achieve the success that you want to achieve. That's because your job is know the success you want and be the only one to achieve it. You're unique in a way that your desires are yours alone, and you're the only person that can achieve what you desire.

I really recommend having a notebook just for your goals. It can be goals you can achieve today or it can be goals you can achieve within 25 years. Create a Master List of your goals. I have my book and it's always fun and feels good to cross things out. Start the book with writing 100 or more things you would like to be, do or have in your life within 25 years. As you write, keep in mind that nothing is impossible. If you can, buy a nice durable, better than average notebook, write down all of your goals. It might take you 1 hour but it will be 1 hour that will bring you the most return on investment.

Be Unstoppable!

As you start setting goals and start having thinking about your goals more often, you will have 2 major obstacles that you will have to overcome every time they try to stop you from achievement. The biggest problem you'll have is the person in the mirror. It's you. You will have fear, you will have limitation in knowledge, you will have doubt, worry, you'll put yourself down, you'll say "this is impossible." The important part is don't let your old self, stop the new and improved you.

As you start taking efforts to achieve your goals your old subconscious programming will be one of the major obstacles It will not be comfortable doing new things. You're subconscious programming might be in the thinking pattern of "Every time I try to achieve a goal, I never achieve it. So that's why I don't even set goals, so I don't disappoint myself.". But when you overcome this obstacle with meditation and positive expectations you will start taking action. When you start taking action and start seeing results, you'll definitely start to also make changes in your subconscious mind.

Rather than talking yourself out of taking effort to achieve your goal, talk yourself into it. Let me repeat that you get it in your head. Don't talk yourself "Out of" taking effort, talk yourself "Into" taking effort. I know some people through casual conversation talk about all their business ideas and after they talk about the ideas, I always say why don't you start taking action on it? Thcy usually say something like "Yeah, but it won't work, or I'm busy doing something else".

My suggestion for people who have business ideas is, don't talk about it unless you're working on it. I used to be talking about my ideas, and it was sometimes to people who would just look for flaws in it and say it won't work. I worked on them anyway. Sometimes they worked out, sometimes they didn't, but you never know if you don't try. So, if you talk about business ideas to people who really can't help you with it, you'll either get some discouragement, flaw finding, or they'll laugh at it. Another reaction maybe positive, they'll tell you to go for it. Either way no one can help turn your ideas into reality but yourself. Don't let yourself stop yourself from achievement. Don't be your worst enemy, be your best friend.

Another part that might attempt to stop you from achieving your goals is the outside circumstances. It can be financial, government regulations, processing difficulties, or location. If you don't have the resource, be resourceful, if there's regulations, find an expert who can help you overcome what needs to be done to get to your goal. If you're not in the right location, do what you need to do to get to the right place to achieve your goals.

I'm not even talking about the haters or people who

discourage you, because those people only affect you if you keep them in your head. So, don't even consider them as outer obstacles That's an inner battle you need to win. You can only win that by having dominant thoughts of love and goals and no negative thoughts at all.

Your outer obstacles might be money. List down as many ways as possible for you to get the money you need. Start taking action on the list until you can get the money you need. Anytime you need money all you have to do is spend less money, and make more money. It's a simple formula that is also coupled with time management. Stop using up your time spending money, and stop using your time not making money.

If you're watching TV 3 hours a day and your complaining that you don't have enough money, that's because you're wasting your time. There are 3 things you could be doing. Learning how to make more money, creating something that can make money in the future, or making money in the moment. If you're able to make money while you're sleeping and have more than enough, then you can go back to watching 3 hours of TV a day.

Anytime you have a list of goals you want to achieve, you will always have obstacles in your way. If there's no obstacles in your way, then your goals are too small. It's better to go for big goals and fail, then to aim small and hit. The biggest obstacles are within you, there will be obstacles outside of you. The best thing you can do is list down the possible obstacles that might hinder you from achievement, and create a bigger list of how you're going to overcome these obstacles Keep in mind that you must be unstoppable. You might have to slow down sometimes, but never stop, always keep going.

About Achievements

When you achieve the goals that you want in life you will have great feelings about all the external things you have. You 'll have the money, the cars, the houses, and live in luxury. These things are great, but it's not your greatest reward. The greatest reward is going through metamorphosis and becoming the ideal person you want to be. You can never have new and better things unless you become a new and better person.

For anyone to have new and better things in life, they always have to take new action, gain new knowledge, and have a new attitude. Eventually all these new things synchronize and become a new way of life. They take effortless action, easily solve problems because of knew knowledge, and keep an attitude of "I can achieve better and bigger things". When you begin the cycle of achievement, you'll always want to achieve more because it will be your way of life.

Taking Small Steps

Sometimes when we set our life goals, we get overwhelmed of all the things that we need to do to get done. Take your large goals and chunk them down into small tasks. After you decided what you want and have measurable goals and deadlines you can take small steps to begin your path to achievement.

Sometimes we don't know what steps to take first. So, it's important you learn how to research through Google, books, online tutorials, or any credible resource that can help you. If you ask a non-expert for advice you might start out taking the wrong steps. The second source of valuable information should be from someone who's already done what you want to do. Ask those people and they'll give good advice on your first steps.

Mind-mapping is something that I do all the time, at least a few times a week, at one point every day. It's a good way of seeing the big picture of your strategy without getting overwhelmed Here's how I do my mind maps

Step 1 – I start out with a circle in the middle of the page. Let's this is my major goal or project.
Step 2 - Then I make circles connected to the main circle. These other circles are major parts of the strategy I need to get done. This can be called my milestones.
Step 3 - I write lines outside of the milestone circles which are tasks I need to complete in order to finish the milestones
Step 4 – I put as much as I can do on my daily to do list and start taking action
Step 5 – I cross out what I finished or add anything that needs to be added as I continue.
Step 6 – Keep going until the major goal or project is finished.

Google Search "Mind Map", you'll see what it looks like.

Most Important Tasks First

Many of us are more energized in the first part of the day. A lot of successful people wake up 4am, workout, get some work done, breakfast with loved ones, and then work hard the whole day. I'm not sure about everyone, the time of day I have the most energy is in the morning. It varies what time in the morning. So, it makes sense for me, to get the most important thing done first thing in the morning.

Try as much as possible, to get the most important thing you need to do throughout the day finished, first thing in the morning. It should a thing that, if you only did that one thing you would still feel good about yourself throughout the day. It might be something for work, or a project that you'll profit from in the future. It might be working out, studying, meditating. It should be something related to your major goals.

In my life working out, reading, and meditating is already part of my morning routine. So, the major tasks that I need to get done first are business related, writing projects, video editing, business strategies, preparing speeches, anything that is related to my major goals. It's great to do the most beneficial thing in the morning even if it's the most difficult. You'll feel good about getting it done, making progress, and it sets the tone for of achieving for day.

The beautiful part about this world is almost everything in the world has already been done. Success is really just a simple formula, it's just difficult to do in the beginning So a way to speed up getting the results you want is find someone who has already done what you want to do. There are so many books, audio courses, and videos on how to be successful. You can start looking for someone who's already successful, contact them and ask for advice.

Internal Dialog of Success

So much of our success is dependent on what we say to ourselves. If our internal dialog is always about limitation, fears, and avoiding risks, we won't get far in life. How far you get in life depends on your confidence and your confidence is dependent on the quality of your internal communication. The negative things you say about yourself to others, comes from a negative internal dialog. One of the first clues to know if you have a good or bad internal dialog is what you say about yourself to others.

One of the best tools that I used to get out of my negative self-talk was affirmations. I used to put myself down all the time, and limited what was possible. In the start of my journey of success, I used to talk myself out of trying to achieve things. Little by little I started trying, but then I would give up, or talk myself out of finishing my projects. I never really thought of myself as successful, so I needed up sabotaging myself all the time. Affirmations really helped me change my internal dialog.

Get rid of yourself fulfilling prophecies. These are the things that you say about yourself that limit you on what you think is possible. Yourself talk becomes yourself image, then yourself image is connected with your confidence, your confidence measures your ability to perform. If you tell yourself "I'll never succeed in business" then a business opportunity comes your way, and you take it but you fail. You'll go back to affirm yourself "See, I told you I'll never succeed in business".

If your mind is always complaining then you'll only get more of what you complain about. You'll attract it with your vibration, and when an opportunity comes along for you to get out of the things your complaining about, you'll be subconsciously programmed to reject it, so you can stay in your comfort zone of complaining. It's time to start focusing on the things you want in life, the more you focus on what you want, think about it, talk about it, write in your journal about it, the closer you bring into manifestation.

Feel the Pain and Keep Going

If people know how hard I work to get what I have, most

people wouldn't even put in any effort. Behind all of my achievements in business, in creative products, my health, and good relationships is a lot of learning, training myself, practicing, failing, failing, and more failing. To get the things I want in life I'm willing to pay the price, whatever it takes. As long as I'm the only one to feel the pain.

In everything that you pursue you always have to pay a price for it. You always have to sacrifice one thing for the other. Right now, it's 4:30 in the morning. I was up since 3AM. I did spend an hour strategist my website before I drank coffee. I was about to go to the gym, but something inside said to work on my book. I'll still go to the gym later this morning. I can't sacrifice going to the gym, but I can sacrifice Social Media browsing. So, I'm writing this book right now at 4:30 in the morning. What were you doing at 4:30 this morning?

There's a lot of things that are needed for you to reach your goals. The main thing is to be willing to feel the pain sacrifice what you know you need to in order to reach your goals. Know that whatever pain you feel is only temporary, the good thing is the benefits will be long term or even timeless.

Think of all the great people in the world you know. All the athletes, like Michael Jordan, he was always the first one in the court and the last one out. Anyone who has ever achieved anything noteworthy spent countless hours trying to reach their goals. Most Billionaires work way more than 8 hours a day, Millionaires also.

Be willing to sacrifice YouTube, Social Media, Entertaining browsing, radio, cheesy novels, gossip, clubbing, or even vacations. Know what you have to sacrifice and know what work you have to put in, feel the pain, enjoy the pain if you can, keep going. Do the work you love is good, but even if you love your work, there will be times it will be painful to keep going. In any case, it's boils down to getting the results you love.

Talent is cheap. Everyone has talent. The difference between talented people and successful people is the amount of work that successful people do. They're willing to put in the time and the effort to get what they want. They're willing to sacrifice. There's a lot of talented people addicted to drugs, so they're main goal for the day is to get high, they never take any effort to cultivate God's gifts.

Know what you want to do, know what you have to sacrifice to get what you want. Keep in mind never sacrifice your health, good relationships, or anything great in your life. Just know that in the beginning there's a big chance you won't be doing as good as you think. But if you keep going, you'll be great at what you do.

Asking Never Hurt No One

You never know until you try, you also will never get unless you ask. Asking is one of the reasons why most people never get the success they want. They're afraid to ask for what they want, from the people who can give it to them. You might be afraid to ask for money from possible investors, time from someone who could help you, or even just asking for information about a possible client.

Let's first figure out why are most people afraid to ask? It might be they're afraid to look greedy, desperate, stupid, or afraid to feel the feeling of rejection. Most people are afraid to get rejected. What you need to realize is if you don't ask, you never get an answer, and by not getting an answer the answer will always be no. So, you get an automatic rejection by not asking.

Start considering who you need to ask something from in order for you to reach your goals. You might need to ask for a loan, a raise, or ask for help with completing a project. You might need to ask someone how you're performing as an employee, a boss, a parent or as a person. You might need to ask a client for referrals or ask someone to help you with a charity. Sometimes asking the right person the right question can change your life.

When you start having the courage to ask people. You will be rejected time to time, or most of the time. Keep in mind that rejection is only a reaction that you choose. If someone says no to you it doesn't mean you've been rejected. It just means they said no to what you asked for. The beautiful part about this is you never really lose anything. If you ask for a raise and your boss say no. You don't lose anything. At least when you have the courage to ask, there's a possibility of gaining something

Every successful person who changed the world has faced rejection. Yet they never gave up on their dream, the preserved themselves. They had a desire and belief in themselves and kept trying after they've been told "No" hundreds and thousands of times. After they heard "no" they said "Next". They just want failure to failure but kept a positive mind until they became successful. You can do the same.

Let Feedback Make You Better

Because I take action all the time, I always get feedback from people. Some are good, some are not. The feedback is good so you know what to improve. Not only from others

I also evaluate myself and do SWOT analysis on myself every quarter. Sometimes it's more useful to know what you're doing wrong, so you can make changes and adjustments needed to improve.

When you start going for your goals, there will be people in the sideline telling you what they think and trying to give you advice. As with anything in life, advice or suggestions can come from negative or positive intentions. Our positive feedback may come in the form of more money, people telling you how great you are, or an inner sense of happiness. For me number one is happiness. If you're not happy, that's feedback that you have to change some things to become happy.

Negative feedback happens all the time so we have to overcome criticism, bad results, getting fired, not getting the outcome you wanted, complaining about life, negative feelings like loneliness, sadness, anger, rage, or feeling like a failure. These negative feedback's in life, should be enough to open your eyes and let you know that change and improvement is needed. Never get comfortable with having negative feedback.

Start viewing negative feedback in your life as a signal to improve. You can improve yourself, your behavior, the way you think, your knowledge, your work ethic, yourself image or self-discipline. You might need to study more, you might have to practice meditation, patience, exercise, learn more, open your mind to bigger and better possibilities in life. Every time you spot negative feedback just ask right away "How can improve myself to eliminate this negative feedback?"

Since there's positive and negative feedback, there will always be a positive or negative reaction to feedback. The first thing to avoid is reacting negatively towards feedback. Some negative reactions maybe wanting to quit, or feeling like a loser. Sometimes feedback makes us feel stuck in the same place or even trapped. Avoid getting angry also. Don't get mad at the people who are giving you feedback that you might not like. Anger always brings negative results. Another thing is not to ignore the feedback. Listen to the feedback, and if there's anything you can change then start making the change.

Anytime you have feedback think of it as an opportunity to learn and to improve. Never make excuses why you're getting negative feedback, rather accept if you haven't been doing the right things, figure out the solutions and make the corrections needed until you get the results you want. Not all feedback might be accurate or useful, so take that into consideration as well.

Kaizen

Do your best to improve yourself every single day. There are so many things we can improve on from our health and fitness, skills, thoughts, relationships, work ethics, discipline. So many things we can improve on. Kaizen is a Japanese word meaning constant and never-ending improvement. It's a philosophy that a lot of successful people and great companies live by. All achievers and champions believe in never ending improvement.

You don't have to take giant steps every day. It's better to take small improvements. Just improve 1 percent each day. You can spend a little more time changing your behavior, improving your relationships, improving your business, organizing, writing, designing, just take small steps. Trying to make a big improvement in one day can take the life out of you, then you won't feel mentally or physically drained the next day and won't take any action.

The important part of Kaizen is Consistent. Without consistency you're just going up and down with improvements. With consistency you're making incremental improvements each day. So, it's important for you to make it a daily routine. Constant means you're always looking for something to improve, this is why feedback is good, because you'll have your eyes open on what to improve. Never ending just means you'll be improving daily, for your whole life. I have a phrase on my wall it's "Always Improving".

If you want to start to make constant and never-ending improvements choose 5 things you should spend more time and effort on when it comes to improving. Make a genuine effort daily to improve on these 5 things. You'll have to spend more time on these 5 things, think more about these 5 things and find ways to improve on these 5 things.

Second part of improving is spending less time on things that really have no benefit and destructive. Even if you're not a drug addict or alcoholic, I'm sure you have bad habits that are just time wasting, and negative thought patterns that are counterproductive. So, list 5 things you need to stop spending time on. Some of these things might be Social Media, checking your phone, YouTube, thinking negative for others, negative self-talk, criticizing others. What are the 5 things you need to spend less time on or eliminate from your life?

Persistence is Essential

This is probably one of the most common traits when it

comes to people who achieve success. It's important that you keep going after the goal you have in mind. The longer you keep trying the more likely you'll be able to achieve what you want. A lot of times people just give up because they think that there's no pot of gold at the end of the road.

There will always be ups and downs and there will be successes and failures. All you have to do is keep going. Even when we plan everything to go perfectly, there's going to be something that we didn't expect would happen to try to stop us or slow us down. So, we need to make sure we keep going after our goals even if obstacles are in our way. Sometimes the Universe will give us challenges to test us on how bad we really want to achieve what we want.

Obstacles are good in a way that they allow us to be creative and be more resourceful. They make us stronger and teach us lessons. There's a saying that where there is crisis there is opportunity. So anytime you have a crisis, it's your opportunity to grow and bring something out of you that hasn't been used yet.

Do More Than What They Expect

A lot of times people around you will expect of you less than you're capable of. Even the expectations you have of yourself might not be that high compared to what you're truly capable of. It's time that you raise the bar higher and expect more from yourself. When at ever you expect of yourself you will get.

If you have a goal of going on a diet, but in the beginning, you tell yourself you're going to fail eventually then you expect yourself to fail. But if you begin the diet with great expectations and hold yourself to higher standards than you'll also get what you expect in a positive way.

Avoid Toxic People

If you spend time with four broke, people, you'll be the fifth. Whoever you spend the most time with you end up being like them. Whatever energy dominates the group you'll be in harmony with that energy. If you spend time with a group of people that criticize other people, then you're in a group full of critics, and it's not going to get you closer to your goals the more time you spend with them.

I always suggest to my clients that anytime there's someone toxic around you, just avoid them completely. If you can't avoid them, know that when two opposing forces are in the same area, let's say within 100 feet of each other, then the dominating force will always win. If a person or people you hang around with are negative, then you'll get sucked into that negativity also. So as much as possible, get away from them.

You can tell when a crowd or workplace is negative when people are always sick. Negative people often times get sick easily. If you're working in a place, and people have permanent illnesses or are on some kind of medication, that's an indication of a toxic environment. When you listen to them talking, if it's about other workers or something negative they heard from the news, or especially if they talk bad about a neighbor of theirs that you don't even know. That's an indication of toxic people.

Gossipers are the most negative people you can ever be around. Avoid these types of people completely. One of the reasons why gossipers are negative is because they talk about people and things they can't change. They're way of feeling like they achieved something is by saying bad stuff about other people. They feel they're better than the people they talk about.

I'll be fair though; a lot of toxic people are just on autopilot from childhood they were raised around gossipers and complainers. From childhood they witnessed their parents, aunts, uncles, neighbors, even schoolmates, gossip, complain about something in the news, talk about crisis. So, they think that talking about problems and negative things in life with other people is a form of bonding with them.

The worst groups are a group of friends or coworkers, or clubs that just talk about problems, and talk negative about other people. The worst of the worst are those groups that compete about who's problem is worse. Like saying to one another "I got more problems than you, you're so lucky." Then the other person takes being called lucky as an insult, or being uncool for the group and responds "I'm lucky? I'm not lucky, actually I have way more problems than you, so I have more problems."

It's time to erase in your subconscious mind that talking about problems or gossiping, is not a form of bonding. Yes, for toxic people, these kinds of conversations are a form of bonding. So, for you to be successful you need to avoid spending time with toxic people as much as possible. If you don't want to let go of spending time with people who are toxic, try to implant a set of standards of positive subjects. There's a saying that great people talk about their plans, average people talk about themselves, and negative people talk about others.

There's a study that said that if you're at least 100 feat away from a toxic person you're as good as being in different countries. Because all of us are vibrating positive and negative energy all the time, if you're always near the toxic person, no matter how positive you make yourself, there are always times that you'll get sucked into the negativity. So, Stay away from them.

If you haven't truly mastered being positive all the time then it's better takes this advice and get rid of all the toxic people from your life. Then find positive and successful people you can spend time with. These people will help you reach your goals and will push you to be better. Successful people usually want to see the best of you spring forth. They want you to spread your wings and fly.

Give yourself Some Praises

The average person has more memories of failing and not achieving than they have of succeeding. It's time to do the opposite. It's time to magnify your successes, glorify even. You will have less confidence each day when you keep reminding yourself of your successes. Most people think about the times they failed and the people that caused it, if they caused the failure than they kick themselves in the butt over it.

It's time to give yourself a high five each day and remind yourself of all the times you succeeded. One way is to first, stop looking for faults of other people. It starts here, when you observe other people and all you do is look at their faults and failures, spending too much time sympathizing with them. Then you're going to connect with the failure part of them. When you look at yourself, you're already on autopilot fault finding.

Start noticing the success of other people say to yourself "Wow that guy used to be broke, now he's so rich. Good for him." Don't say things like "Wow that woman is now rich, but she's from a rich family anyway, that's why she's rich." Don't take credit away when you praise someone for their success. Give them all or even more credit than they deserve, because you really don't know what they been through in order for them to reach success.

When it comes to yourself remember all of the success you had, even in grade school. You can start from as young as you can remember, and then continue through stages of your life, from grade school, to high school, to teenage years, your twenties, mid-twenties, or thirties. Whatever age you might be now, just every 5 years write down all the successes you've had. It might be academic, financial, creative, overcoming obstacles or fears, relationships, it can be internal success or external success. Write them all down in a piece of paper to remind yourself.

If you had any achievements like diplomas, certificates, or if you were in the newspaper, you wrote a book, you made a music album. You worked for a famous person and took a picture with them; you can put all of your achievements on the walls of your house. It can be anywhere. It's nice if it's everywhere, so that wherever you are in your house you are reminded of your successes. Your physical environment creates great mental triggers. Your walls a great place for you to have inspiration of some sort. If you put things on your wall and there's a lot of space left, put some motivational art on your wall to inspire you daily.

Stay Focused on Your Goals

Another difference between successful people and failures is that failures keep changing their minds on what they want. They switch goals, or they decide not to take action on their goals. They postpone the work. Successful people are always thinking about their goals, they even obsess about goals. Every single day they stay focused on the goals they have.

It's easy to stop trying when you get discouraged, it takes a lot of work and effort to stay positive no matter what's going on in your life. It takes will power to continue on even when the road is difficult. For successful and positive people, they stay focused on what they want to achieve and take actions daily so they get one step closer.

One of the most important ways to stay focused is to take time planning and reviewing your plans. A lot of times we have plans, but we never take action on them. Take 30 minutes to even one hour each day if it's morning or night time. Usually it's good night time, so before you sleep your plans will rest in your subconscious mind.
Write about how you can improve, what mistakes you might have made and decide to never make the same mistake again. Write what you could have done better or actions you could have taken. What actions can you take tomorrow? You can also write about what kind of life you want to live in the long term. What things or people you need to eliminate from your life, and what can you add or do more of for you to succeed in achieving your goals.

Finish What You Started!

When you start projects, businesses or attempt to learn or master a new skill. Keep going until it's done! Many people failures are fickle in their decisions on what road to take in life. They begin learning a new skill like cross fit, and they enjoy it in the beginning, but eventually they either get bored or start fearing the pain of working out.

They start making excuses, then they try another workout regime like running, then quit that also.

Have you ever started a project and stopped 25% or 50% towards its completion? Like writing a book is one of the most common projects people give up on. What are the reasons you stopped? Those excuses are the ones stopping you from achieving. I understand we can only pay attention to so many things at one time, but when you have unfinished work, this takes up space in your mind and will make you less effective in many other things.

When you have unfinished work, your mind stops in the middle of doing something else and thinks about the unfinished work. Then you start going into this cycle of feeling less than, or guilty about not finishing your work. The guilt of having unfinished work should be enough to motivate you to continue. Or maybe you need to work on scheduling your time to finish your projects, or write a plan to get over an obstacle that might have hindered you from working on your projects.

One of the ways to get your projects finished is if you can get someone else to work on it, delegate it. If it's something that you can do yourself then do it. Then if it's something that doesn't really need to be done right now, but you're sure it should be done, schedule it for a future date then make sure you work on it eventually. If you think that the project's not worth your time and has no return in investment, then forget about it.

One way to make sure you get things done in every form of life is to discipline yourself in your skill. Everything carries over to everything else. Usually if you're disciplined in something you have passion for, you're also disciplined at many things your passionate about. If you're passionate about your goals, you'll find discipline to achieve them. Whatever your passionate about, work on being disciplined in that thing. If you're passionate about singing, discipline yourself to be a good singer, or a good song writer. Discipline yourself to learn to edit music. Discipline yourself to gain skills and overcome obstacles to finish your projects.

Don't Run from Pain Go Towards It

Many people live in denial. They think that they're perfect, they think they're always right. They think they're better than others, when things aren't going well, they won't' admit it. People make excuses about having bad relationships, they make excuses and blame others for their financial situation. They make mistakes but never admit it. They lie to themselves about their flaws and lack of ability. Some people just have a false sense of confidence. They have confidence but they're not competent.

Sometimes people make up reasons why things aren't working in business. Many times, we're just afraid to face the truth. Like if you sense your worker is stealing something, or you already caught them lying to you, but you don't want to confront them or take corrective action, eventually the problem will get bigger. They'll think they can get away with lying and just keep lying about small things and big things.

For most people it's in their diet. They're eating too much sugary food, drinking too much soda and they tell themselves that they're actually eating an average amount. Or they tell themselves "This is my last cake". Eventually they'll see signs of weight gain or have health issues.

Same with people who don't want to face the truth that they have a drinking problem or smoking problem. They might not see major signs right away, but the minor signs will be there. They might not perform well at work, they'll have hangovers. If they smoke, they'll run out of breath, or become too dependent on cigarettes mentally, that every time they have a problem, they spend 5 minutes smoking a cigarette and worry about the problem.

You can also face the truth in your thinking, emotions and actions. If your life isn't going well, you might not be treating people well, you might not have the dominating thoughts and good feelings for yourself and others, you'll see clues in your life that it's not the way you want it to be. If your finances aren't going well it means you need to fix your income or your spending. If your relationships aren't going well, you need to fix your giving and receiving love.

Do a check up on yourself, before you need a psychologist to do it for you. Be truthful to yourself and list down everything in your life that's not going your way. Find the root cause to this problem. Be determined to eliminate the root cause, if it's your thinking, lack of action, or even avoiding people. List different solutions you can take action on to start taking action on to get rid of the root cause, so that this area of your life will go as you want it.

Positive Beliefs Only

The Law of life is belief. What you believe about yourself will make you limited or limitless. What you believe about others you will get from them. If you believe the world is a cruel place then people in the world will be cruel to you. Even if they intend to be nice, you'll find a way to be what you want them to be. If you believe everyone's always angry, you'll find a way to make them angry.

Most people intend to have positive beliefs but really have negative beliefs. Most people have beliefs that really limit the amount of success they should be enjoying. No matter how hard you try to be successful, your subconscious mind is programmed that success is out of your reach, then you'll never be successful.

We have beliefs about everything ingrained in our mind from childhood and everything we've experienced. We have beliefs about money, about people, the world as a whole, about our beauty, our brains, our capabilities, our limitations, other people's limitations. Not all of them are positive believes. Many beliefs are negative beliefs. These beliefs become part of our inner dialog and way of thinking.

When it comes to health, many people never become truly healthy because they believe working out is tiresome. The believe it's too expensive to join a gym, when really people spend more from not working out because they end up in the hospital for illnesses once a year. What you believe about living a healthy lifestyle might be negative.

Most people believe that money is bad, and wanting money is bad. They think that they'll never get financially successful because they never saw anyone get rich when they grew up. They believe rich people are evil, so when they try to become rich, they sabotage themselves. They believe having too much money is greedy so they don't want to have too much. They believe money is all about borrowing because they saw their parents borrow money all the time, they end up borrowing money all the time also.

When it comes to relationships people have negative beliefs

that if you're not fighting in your relationship than it's not a good relationship, actually fighting is not a necessity of a good relationship. Or they believe that everyone is in it for themselves, and end up saying "I'll be in it for myself too then", then try to rip people off. They believe that everyone's fake, so they never get too close to anyone, and end up lonely.

There's a lot of areas in life that you might have negative beliefs on. There's politics, religion, society, the government, people at work, your boss, your workers, your luck, your capabilities. Maybe it's time to list down all your negative beliefs about everything you can think of. Start with negative beliefs about yourself, money, health, relationships and your capabilities. Start with every negative belief that impacts your life right away. Then you can list down your negative beliefs about the world.

After you write all your negative beliefs, especially the beliefs that are stopping you from reaching your goals, write where did this belief come from? Did it come from a gossiping neighbor? Did it come from your parents or friends? Something you saw on the internet? After that write down how this belief is actually a false belief. Write new belief that might be a total opposite of the negative belief, or at least something positive that you can replace the negative belief with. Then every time you think of the negative belief, automatically repeat the positive belief for one minute. So, you crush that negative belief out of your subconscious with repeated affirmations.

Clarity is so Important

It's very important that you get a clear picture of how you want your life in the future. Get clear on exactly how much money you want to make, how you intend to make that money. You should get clear in the house you want to live in, the car you want to drive, the people you want to be living with, the work you want to have. In simple terms get clear in the environment you want to sleep, wake up, and spend your waking hours in.

Clarity in what you want doesn't really have to be work only. It can be just activities you want to be doing. A lot of women's life dream is to marry someone they truly love and be a house wife for their children. After that they become a good Grandmother for their children. It's like the Ikigai, which means "The reason they jump out of bed in the morning."

When it comes to money you should be clear on the amount of money you want to have in your life. At first, and only at first, you might not have to know how you'll get the money. If you depend on luck and winning the lottery to get the money, there's a big chance you'll never get it. The Law of Compensation states, in order to get something, you have to give something. You have to make it clear on the amount of money you want, and have a clear plan of getting that money.

One of the reasons why clarity is very important is because the more detailed it is in your mind, the faster the gestation period. This gestation period will only be sped up by the deepness of your faith that you'll get what you want in life. The deeper you believe and experience something to be real the faster that thing will come to you.

Even in practical thinking people who don't understand the Universal Laws this makes total sense. The more vivid you can imagine your goal being achieved, and how you're able to achieve it. The more confidence you'll have in taking action. The more action you take towards a goal, the faster you'll be able to get your goal. Even if your plan isn't perfect, you'll be able to make adjustments needed after making mistake and failures. Just know that every wrong decision is a step closer to making the right decision. As long as you learn from your short comings and keep going.

Don'ts of Clarity

Sometimes for whatever reason, we don't get what we want in life. If you're not clear on what you want, you'll definitely get mixed results. Sometimes we set a goal, but don't take enough action. Instead of taking more action, we just change the goal. Eventually changing goals becomes a cycle. They keep changing goals, because they don't take enough action. So, by always changing goals they get mixed results.

When it comes to clarity in your visualization, you don't really have to see everything in detail. One of the most important things is to feel the feeling of having what you want. Sometimes clarity in feeling is enough for you to get what you want. I, myself am not very visual when I visualize, it takes me some time to get everything in detail. For some people they can get everything in detail in a few seconds or minutes. For some people like me I need to get the feeling first, then I can start getting the vision in detail.

So, you might not be able to get what you want in visual details, but if you can get clear in emotional intensity it can help you attract what you want in life. Your thought, feelings and actions help get you what you want. The clearer the thought, through visualization, the deeper clarity in feeling, and clarity in what actions to take is very important in attracting the things you want in life.

Focus on What You Want Only

I'm not sure what's going on with people these days. I have friends, family that are adults and I guess not a lot of people practice focusing on what they want in life. Most people think they're above average in thinking, and they think positively, but they don't. Mostly everyone pays way too much attention on what is.

People pay way too much attention on everything they see. Most people focus on what is, and what's bad about what is. For example, I sometimes have people in my car that don't practice The Law of Attraction. When we're driving from one place to another all they focus on is "Look at that old building", "Look at that crazy person." "What's that?" "That girl shouldn't be wearing that shirt." "Why doesn't the government do something about this road?" "That guy looks dangerous" "What's that girl doing with that ugly guy. She can do better than that.". "Oh my God, there's an accident. Stop, let's take a look. Oh My God! There's blood! I'm scared!" Their just in the car, paying attention to everything outside the car, they use their thought energy, emotions, and attention to pay attention to what is. Any emotion they feel about what is, are emotions they created.

Imagine how much energy your wasting? How much thought energy, emotional energy? Always keep in mind that any emotion we feel is an emotion we created. We think we feel these emotions as a fault of someone or something outside of us. For higher conscious beings, we know that all emotion within us is created by us. When you continuously focus on what's in front of you physically, and wasting your energy speaking about it, feeling emotional about it, and thinking about it. You're plain old wasting your energy!

So, one of the ways to change the way you think is not to react to what is. Yes, you see two drunk guys fighting while driving home. What's the point of telling your friend "Hey I saw two drink guys fighting on the way home"? What good will it do for your friend? What good will it do for you? It will only do bad, it will only put you in a sense of danger. You'll just have an emotional feeling that this place is dangerous.

Understand that most people spread bad news with an intention to either look cool, or be the "I'm the first one who knew about the bad news. Remember I'm the first one that told you?" If your intention is try to impress people with bad news. It's basically a cheap way to have an ego boost. You're just trying to make yourself feel good by spreading something bad. Not only is it a cheap way to boost your ego, it also has a negative karmic consequence. Though shall not kill, but you're killing someone's positive mood with negative news.

Another downfall of many people who could never focus on what they want in life is they're too busy criticizing other people. They walk to the bust stop to take the bus, they criticize the fat girl waiting, saying "I hope she doesn't sit next to me and take up half my seat". When they get inside the bus, they criticize the group of real estate agents talking loud about trying to close a sale. This person is wasting thought energy to criticize in his head saying "If they had enough real estate sales, they wouldn't be here taking the bus." Not realizing they're on the same bus, so they're probably making the same amount of money.

When they get off the bus and go to work, after a year working in the same office, they already have a list of people they like, and dislike. Then they criticize co-workers in their head like "This bastard, better not try to say hi to me" They then talk to their boss and criticize the boss in their heads as well. All they're doing is criticizing people, movie stars, people on the news, anything and everyone they can criticize they waste thought energy creating a criticism and expressing it. And that's not focusing on what you want in life.

Criticizing is one of the biggest wastes of thought energy. That's why it's important to practice non-judgement. Non-judgement helps you to accept people as they are, accept the world as it is, accept your situation as it is and just continue to focus on what you want in life. When you start to eliminate your opinions about everyone and everything, you have more energy to focus on what you want in life. When you stop wasting emotions on what you don't like in life, you have more emotional strength to focus on what you love.

Nothing Else

One of the surest ways to get anything you want in life is to focus on what you want and nothing else. That's the simplest formula's to getting what you want. What you focus on expands. The depth of intensity and emotion you give and the amount of time spent focusing on what you want in life creates a bigger tube in a way, or faster connection.

It's like watching YouTube in a way. If you're watching YouTube on your WIFI and you're not in any other website and aren't doing anything else with your computer than your YouTube video will play super-fast with no problem. If you're watching YouTube, then you're on Facebook in another browser, playing a game in another browser and watching Netflix in another browser. Your YouTube video might play then stop, then play then stop, then play, then stop.

Same as when you're trying to manifest something in life. You're trying to finish a website for your business, but you still have to make money so you have to work, then you still have to spend time with your kids, then your friends want you to come out for someone's birthday, then you still need to work out also. Then someone offers you money for a quick project with a deadline, so you have to put your website aside. Then your favorite TV Show is on every 9pm, so you can't work on your website that time. If you really wanted your website done, you would focus only on your website and nothing else.

As long as it doesn't damage you financially or doesn't do damage in other areas of your life you might have to sacrifice time from, then Focus only on what you want, and nothing else. Other than your family, work you need to do to survive, and exercising, everything else is a distraction. If you want to achieve a great and difficult thing, it will take time, energy and concentration. If it's in business, writing a book, being an MMA fighter, becoming a body builder, becoming an astronaut. Other than your family, survival work, and health rituals, everything else is a distraction.

It's good if you can list down everything that's a distraction in your life. You need to do this without emotion. Maybe it's your going out at night that's a distraction, or maybe it's entertainment. Some of the biggest distractions are entertainment, going on social media, hanging out with friends, shopping, there's a lot of things that waste your time.

Alcohol and smoking are a waste of time, too much time on

researching random things on Google. If you read too much like I do, sometimes it can be a waste of time, in a way that I use it to procrastinate. Instead of working on what's most important the first thing in the morning. Sometimes I just end up reading, and postponing the thing I have to do, though whole day. Sometimes meeting with people who don't help you make money is a waste of time. I have good meetings with people that they give me advice and I give them advice. It might have helped in a way, but I realized I could have used that time to do more productive work.

It's a good practice to keep in mind what you notice throughout the day, stop yourself from expressing your opinion about non important things. Even deep inside practice not judging and criticizing people in your mind. Then start to focus only on what your grateful, what makes you happy, what makes you laugh, the people you love, the activities you love to do. Focus only on those good things.

Feeling Wealth into Existence

Money comes to those who feel wealthy already. The majority of people in the Philippines never put true effort to try feeling wealthy. They know how it feels to have money problems and since the feeling of money problems is what they're familiar with, they continue to feel tomorrow what they felt today and yesterday. Poverty consciousness leads to more poverty.

One of the biggest causes of poverty consciousness in the masses of the Philippines is Media. Although there's Media that send positive messages and inspire people. A lot of radio channels and talk shows just talk about the bad news, the crimes, joke about how bad it is to be poor and talk about it's better to be poor. Almost all newspapers in the world put fear articles, like crimes, people getting hurt and crisis. It's the same in the Philippines. Even the internet, bad news gets shared more than good news. You can tell your co-workers or family members are in the Dogma when they repeat negative news and copy opinions of people they hear on the radio.

The feeling of lack, fear, anger, desperation, all of these emotions are somehow connected to each other. When you connect with any negative emotion, you disconnect with positive emotions. Like I said, you can only feel one emotion at a time. So, when your mind is filled with fear of death, fear of poverty, fear of getting robbed while going to work. You'll have no room to feel the good feelings that's needed for you to attract wealth, happiness and prosperity.

There's a truth when they say the richer get richer, and the poorer get poorer. That much leads to more, and those who don't have much, the little they have will be taken away from them. The reason for this truth is when you feel you don't have much, you attract more lack. People who don't have much often complain about how bad their life is, and they can only pay attention to opportunities that keep it that way. When you only pay attention to the poverty in the world, that's all you'll get.

It's time to change the way you think about the world. Recognize that the world is an abundant world, the Philippines is an abundant in resources, in smart people, it's abundant in opportunities for work. The main reason people don't have a job is because they never develop a high paying skill. They think they should get big bucks, but they have small skills. There's really an abundant amount of opportunity in the Philippines to make money if you have the right mindset and skills.

Feeling your way to abundance starts with the understanding that there's an abundance of resources in the world. There's more than enough of everything to go around for everyone. There's enough for everyone in the world to be a millionaire. If all the money and resources were split evenly then everyone would be a millionaire. If you have a millionaire mindset and skills, you'll keep the money. If you think like everyone else, you'll lose the money like most people and go back to your comfort zone of having money problems.

The first part of feeling your way to abundance is Gratitude. I know gratitude has been written about by many people, but hopefully you'll learn enough here to really practice it every day. When you're not grateful, what you have will be taken away from you. You can use gratitude as a defense for you not to lose what you already have. People usually will take more action not to lose P10,000.00 than to make P10,000.00. Think of gratitude as your defense not to lose what you already have.

If you complain "How can I be grateful for what I already have when I don't have much?". Any complaining about what you already have will surely bring you more things to complain about in the future. The feeling you feel now is an indication of what you'll receive in the future. If you're reading this book, then I'm sure you have many things to be thankful for.

Let's start small. Be thankful for the water, coffee, tea, cacao, juice, soda, coconut. Whatever you drank the last 24 hours, be so grateful that you smile. Be thankful for the food you ate, the people you love, the eyes you have, your hands and feet. Thank God for the fresh air your breathing, your electric fan. Thank God for your work, that you went to school. Be thankful for your friends, everyone that ever helped you in life. Be thankful for the last time you laughed. Be thankful your alive, and you have time to change your life for a better tomorrow.

The beautiful thing about gratitude is that it's a form of giving. You give gratitude to God. Your thanking God so you connect with God through gratitude. I've said that every moment of life is a prayer, your emotions, and how you feel is your constant connection to God. Since giving causes receiving, when you give gratitude, you will receive more things to be grateful for. The shortcut to being rich is to be grateful. When you feel grateful, you feel rich, when you feel rich, you get more of what you're feeling.

This is why it's important to avoid complaining. When you complain about not having enough, your giving to God negative energy. Even if you're not praying, your still connected to God, and when you complain you're actually praying for more things to complain about. Even if you're just complaining to yourself or someone you know. If your complaining today, expect more things to complain about in the future. Starting today, replace complaining with gratitude.

To always feel grateful takes work. Don't expect that it will be an easy journey. You have your automatic way of thinking and reacting to the world, so you need conscious awareness in your emotions for you to always be grateful. Affirmations is a good way and make sure you equip yourself with gratitude affirmations.

Don't think that since your thankful today, good things will come automatically. You still have to wash away all the days you've been ungrateful and complaining.

Riding the Law of Attraction Correctly

Some people understand how the Law of Attraction works. That if you think and feel wealthy, you'll become wealthy. Thinking, feeling and speaking about what you want is only a small part of The Law of Attraction. Half of the word Attraction is "Action". Action is the biggest part of attracting what you want in life. The thinking and feeling will only lead you to take the right action.

Other Universal laws need to be understood before making sure The Law of Attraction works in your favor. You need to understand The Law of Cause and Effect and giving and receiving. For you to attract what you want in life you have to give, before you receive. You have to give something of value to people in order for you get money.

There are 3 ways for everyone to receive money that is in line with cause and effect, and giving and receiving. One way is to sell products. You can create a product or you can find a product that people are buying, and be the one to sell it to them. You can provide services like book keeping, graphic designing or any freelance type of service and receive money. You can also sell knowledge, this is training, teaching or writing a book that people are willing to pay for. The more people you can provide products, services or knowledge to, the more income you'll be able to receive.

There's also a blockage that is in the way of people who want money but aren't getting the amount of money they want. People have negative beliefs about money. They believe that money is evil, or money is difficult to receive. When you believe that you have to work hard for money then you'll only attract ways to work hard for money. If you believe that there's not enough money in the world, then you'll only experience not having enough money.

Your money comfort zone can also be something that blocks you from receiving money. If you're only comfortable with P25,000.00 then when you receive P100,000.00 you'll find a way to spend it. You might spend recklessly, go on a vacation, or buy stuff for people until the amount of money you have is more or less P25,000.00. That's why visualization and practicing making yourself feel wealthy is important, to make you feel comfortable with having the amount of money you want. When you start feeling comfortable imagining having the money you want, then when you have the amount of money, you'll be able to keep it.

One time a student asked how she can attract money for her family. I think she just wanted the money to come out of thin air. Without knowing you have to give something of value to get the amount of money. So, I'll just list down ways for students to make money while going to school. Keep in mind in order for you to have enough time to make money while going to school, you have to give up time wasting activities like YouTube, Googling, watching movies, hanging out with friends, Social Media or any other activities that doesn't involve your school or making money.

Here are several ways for students to make money while going to school:

1. Try to do chores for your family and ask for extra money
2. Ask relatives and neighbors if they have any work you can do for them
3. Get a Part Time Job at a Jollibee, Starbucks

or anywhere hiring part time workers
4. Start writing a book and learn how to sell it
5. Buy and sell things to your classmates, like snacks, food or anything they already buy
6. Sell Load
7. Make something people are already buying and sell it to them
8. Join a Network Marketing Company, good for income and for training
9. Increase your skills at something like graphic designing, web developing or writing and find freelance work.
10. Baby Sit for Single Parents

So, the bottom line is you can't get money if you're not helping other people. If you want more money you have to be able to help other people make more money, or make their lives better in some way.

3 Basic Steps of Meditation

In the Philippines not too many people meditate, but it's starting to catch on. One of the surest ways for you to live a great life is to practice meditation. Most successful people meditate, and if they don't meditate, they take walks, which is beneficial to the mind. When you continually practice meditation, you'll eventually become a master of your thoughts. Mastering your thoughts is an essential part of controlling your destiny.

I meditate about 3 times a day. Usually in the morning, before or after lunch and in the night time. There's a lot of wonderful things you can do while meditating. The first and foremost step is to still your body. Which means put your body in a state of relaxation. When your body is in a state of relaxation and calmness you won't feel stressed or any negative emotions. When your body is tense it feels fear. When it's calm it feels love.

After being able to put your body at ease the second important step is to clear your mind. This means clearing the chatterbox that won't shut up. I call it eliminating language. If we never learned language all we would have is emotion and intuition. Sometimes language is a barrier to our intuition. We can all say the words love or happiness, but to feel it without saying the word puts you in a higher level of conscious awareness that most people never tap into.

The third step is to have conscious awareness of how you feel. Without using language make yourself feel as good as you can at that moment. You can make yourself feel love, happy, grateful, bliss or any emotion you wish to choose. This is why meditating is so beautiful, because you will never have to depend on anyone else to make you feel positive emotions. You become 100% in control of how great you want to feel. If you want to feel wealth and abundance you can feel that during meditation.

These three steps are sort of the basic parts of meditation, it's just clearing your mind, thinking nothing, wanting nothing, and choosing your best feelings. When your able do all of these things during meditation, you'll be able to do it throughout the day. So, whatever happens during your day you'll be able to always control what you think and feel.

Meditations that Will Change Your Life

Another great thing that I do during meditation is repeating affirmations. But before repeating affirmations or mantras you have to make sure there's no tension. The best time to repeat affirmations is upon waking up or before sleeping because your subconscious mind is open like soil ready for new seeds. There are different types of affirmations for achieving goals, changing negative beliefs, creating a new self-image, eliminating fears, and replacing negative beliefs. Morning affirmations are great for goal and new positive beliefs.

For example, if you want to have multiple sources of income and more money, at the same time eliminate the negative belief that money is difficult to get. You can say "Money comes to me in extra large quantities, from multiple sources easily and frequently" You can repeat this over and over until the affirmation becomes a feeling. It's also good to mix visualizations with affirmations, so while you repeat an affirmation while you feel it, you can also see it.

Another thing I love to do while meditating is "Experiencing the Life I want to live". This is visualizing my perfect day. Driving my dream car, living in my dream house, doing my life's work with happiness and ease. I might be visualizing myself signing books, or driving to several businesses or just relaxing in a mansion or condo. Traveling with my family, giving talks to thousands of people or performing music. Just visualizing things that I enjoy.

I also do "Love Meditations" Where I just feel love, send love to everyone I know, send love to everything that enters my mind. I just repeat "I love you" for 15 minutes or longer and whatever enters my mind, if it's problems, or people that I care for, and people who might be giving me problems, I still send them love. This is giving great love to God, myself, people I love, all of God's creations, and people who need my forgiveness. This creates a feeling of love in anything I think of.

One meditation that is so powerful for me is "God Meditation". This is being consciously aware of God inside me, and God connected to everything that exist. I can be consciously aware of God without using words, which in turn strengthens my intuition. Or I can say a mantra "Dear God I love you with all of my heart". Then I just keep repeating the words until all I feel is love for God, it feels so good I can feel my spirit and am able to listen to my intuition much easier.

The "The Gratitude Meditation" is one that I do even if I'm not meditating but when I meditate and repeat "Thank You God for All of my Blessings" I really feel gratitude in a deeper level. The gratitude meditation will always make me smile and feel happy. When you consistently practice the gratitude meditation you will eventually receive a continuous flow of blessings as long as your also consciously never feeling fear and always feeling love as you go about your day.

Sometimes when things aren't going right, or I'm spending too much money on things I shouldn't be spending on, I start to feel lack. Anytime I notice myself thinking of lack, I do the "Abundance Meditation" I just repeat "I always have an abundance of money" Then I think about the abundance in the world, about all the wealth there is in the world. I continue the affirmation until worry goes away and all I feel is abundance.

"I Love My Life" Meditation is especially good when you start going into a negative spiral from focusing on what's not working in your life. When your able to repeat "I love my life" over and over until you feel the love you have for your life, you will begin to attract more love into your life. You'll also start to consciously focus on what you love about your life, and this will overshadow the bad. The truth is you're 100% responsible for loving your life.

Different Types of Affirmations

The number one goal for affirmations isn't so much getting the universe to give you what you want. When your intention is using affirmations to try to get the Universe to give you something it sometimes can backfire if you're in a state of want. The feeling of want leads to more want. The number reason you should be doing affirmations is to eliminate negative beliefs in a subconscious level. Once you plant positive beliefs in your subconscious mind you change the core of who you are. We never attract what we want, we attract what we are.

Goal Achieving Affirmations are great because they get you to subconsciously believe that you have already achieved your goal, that your goal is also believable. In order to maximize this, you have to be able to visualize and feel your goal as if it's already achieved. This takes a great deal of imagination, in a way it takes work, because thinking is the most difficult work there is.

Tools You Need for Total Success in Life

When I talk about total success in life it means you should be successful in every part of your life. Some people think that if they're rich they won't be happy, or if they spend time and energy on making money, they don't have time to work out. We all have enough time to have anything and everything we want in life.

It's all a matter of belief. The law of life is what you believe becomes true for you. So, if you believe in limitation than you'll live a life of limitation. When you believe you have unlimited potential then you'll live a life that you can be, do and have anything and everything you ever wanted in life.

Affirmations

Affirmations is a good starting tool for you to use on a daily basis. In my experience I use different types of affirmations through the day. The main point for all affirmations is to change your subconscious beliefs. It's to replace negative beliefs with positive beliefs. In techno lingo it's to re-program the algorithm of your mind so it may be more effective at living your best life.

One type of affirmation is to change your subconscious belief about the goals you're aiming to achieve. Let's say you have a goal of having P1,000,000.00 by the end of the year. All you have to do is write down your goal in a paragraph as if you've already achieved it. It's OK if you don't know how you'll get the money, but it's better if you can put somewhere in your paragraph how you'll get the money. You can put a date but just knowing it's within the year is fine. Sometimes putting a date makes people feel pressured.

An example is "Thank you God that I have P1,000,000 in my bank account". Then you just repeat it first thing in the morning and last thing at night. The most important part is getting the emotion of having P1,000,000. How does having P1,000,000 feel? Don't use your mind, feel it right now. Don't think of spending it, just feel the feeling of having it.

A lot of people say visualize having it, but for me I would start with the feeling of having it. In the beginning process of changing your subconscious beliefs for me, the feeling is the most important part. This means being able to feel having what you want, without words. Visualization is important in achieving your goals, but for the beginning part, start with repeating an affirmation of what you want, until you don't have to say the words anymore, you just feel the feeling.

As much as you can throughout the day feel the feeling of having what you want without having to say affirmations. When you have a hard time feeling the feeling of having what you want, keep repeating your affirmation until you feel the feeling again. Your feelings are the closest thing to your soul, which is the closest thing to God.

Types of Negative People to Eliminate

All of us have different types of thoughts. One of the steps towards Conscious living is to eliminate negative thoughts. The bulk of society and people you grew up around are negative thinkers and have negative conversations all the time.

A lot of people think when they talk about their problems with people, it's a way for them to bond. Bonding in this negative way is not good for both parties. When two people come together and talk about negative things in their lives, they multiply more negative things to come. So, the next time they meet they'll talk more negative things.

One thing that works wonders instantly is eliminate negative people from your life. Get rid of all the toxic people. There are different levels of toxic people. Here's a list of what I consider to be toxic people.

Self-Pity Person – These people always have a sad story about how life is unfair, and people are not treating them right, they have problems, they feel sick, they're worried about something. Usually they don't have much ambition in life. Self-pity people always have major health problems, mental issues, relationship problems, work problems. Also, every don't feel good they'll tell whoever they talk to.

The Angry Person – This person's always angry about something. They're always angry about the government, people they know, their friends, their family. They get angry about a character in a movie. They just react with anger any chance they get. When you waste your time listening to what makes these people angry, you're really wasting your time, energy and thought into something you have no control over.

The I hope Something Bad Happens to You Person – These people are so pathetic and waste so much energy hoping something bad happens to other people. They hope failure financial, relationship, health or any failure they can think of for other people. Even worse, they go to church and pray for failure or something bad happens to other people. The thing they don't know is if you're wishing bad for others, you're holding that negative energy. Before you can throw a ball at someone, you have to hold the ball in your hand first. These people are stupid because they always end up being the ones that get hurt. If you wish bad things for others, you're vibrating that bad energy. The Universe doesn't know if that energy is for others. It just knows your vibrating that bad energy. So, you'll attract more bad energy.

The Complainer – This is the most common especially among the lower and middle class. They complain about not having enough money, they complain about what someone said, they complain about the car they have, the house they have, the gadget that broke, they complain about the traffic, they complain about people at work, about the work they have to do. They complain about having to drop off their kids. They complain about you being late, about their husband, children, the weather. Anyone that complains about petty things is petty person. They major in minor things, and have a meaningless existence, never finding their true purpose and never live up to their true potential, because they spend too much time complaining.

The Criticizer – This is also common, mostly to the insecure and the people who feel inferior. Criticizing is a childish thing to do. We all learned criticizing during our childhood. Adults criticize us, but mostly children are criticizing children. I think it's more out of fun and laughter before, not for a sense of feeling superior. As we grew up, we learned to criticize to feel equal to people we feel inferior to. Just know that when people criticize you it means they feel inferior to you. Always know that. Reasons people criticize is they're jealous, they feel insecure, they're on auto-critic mode which shows they live a very dissatisfied life. The worse part about people who criticize is they mentally live in hell, because they criticize themselves all the time. The reason many adults lack confidence is because they criticize themselves and others too much.

The Opinionated – Everyone is entitled to their opinion, but the more opinions you speak about the cheaper you are as a person. Why? Opinions are the cheapest thing on earth. Everyone has them, anyone can talk about opinions any time. When you give your opinions all day every day without anyone asking, your filling our lives with useless information. We can't make money with your opinions. We can't enrich our lives with your opinions. It's really no use to anyone what you think about the president, the government, your next-door neighbor, your co-workers, what you think about those shoes, that shirt, or anything. The only time your opinion is useful is if someone asks for it.

The Idea but do-Nothing Person – This person has an idea about an app, a business idea, they have ideas how to get to the moon using a drone. They have all these ideas that might make the world better, but they never do anything about it. If you have a friend that has ideas and works on them than that's good. If they're talking about plans, that's good. Usually the Idea but do-Nothing person has an idea, and when you encourage them to take steps, they'll give you all the reason's they can't work on it. If all they have is ideas they're not working on, then they're not motivated and maybe not productive.

The Discouraging Person – One of the reasons why you should never tell your plans with people is because they'll discourage you, tell you why it won't work, or suggest a "try better goal to aim for", or even worse, "Try a goal that's more achievable". There's the law of Relativity and it means they can't see anything in you that is not within them. So, if they tell you not to aim too high, it's because they haven't been aiming high and that's all they can see in other people.

Plain Old Hater - These people hate their lives so they hate everyone else. You know someone is a hateful person when they have a list of people they hate. You can just feel their hate boiling when you walk by them. These people are the type just to talk about all your mistakes, all your troubles and anything bad they can say about you, they'll start conversations with others about everyone they hate.

The Blamer – This person usually lacks ability in many ways. They lack ability to deal with emotional issues, take responsibility, and lacks ability to solve problems. So, the only thing they can do is blame other people. They blame other people if their relationships don't work out, they blame others if they don't do good at work. They blame others for financial problems. Instead of solving issues or just good old take responsibility, they just blame other people.

Excuses person – This person has all types of excuses why they never made it in life, why they didn't do good in their relationships or career. This person is similar to the blamer but broader. This person uses a lot of excuses at work, like they're late because of traffic, they didn't finish the project because they don't know what to do. They didn't graduate college because of financial issues. One thing I tell my workers is don't give me excuses, find a way to get the result. An excuse is simply an obstacle that can be solved if a person put enough time and energy to solve it.

I'm too High Class – This person can be rich or can be poor even. They think they're too good to go to certain places. They fear criticism to be seen in a certain super market or certain area in town. I've seen people who are born poor and think they're too high class to go somewhere, and there's a lot of rich people who think they're too high class to talk to others or go to certain places. If you fear to be criticized because you're seen in a certain place, it's not that you're too high class. You have fear, and that's negative energy.

I want you to Fear Me Person – This person isn't good for you because they suck the life out of you in a way when you give in to what they want from you. If anyone wants you to fear them, show them that you don't. Once you allow yourself to be controlled by fear, you need to get out of that 137environment if it's professional or personal. If you fear your boss, and you're working in fear most of the time, it's not good for your health. If you're in a relationship and you're staying cause of fear, then get out. Any fear-based relationship is no good for anyone.

The Limited Knowledge Advisor – Never take advice from fools. Just because you ask someone for advice it doesn't mean they'll give good advice; you still have to weigh things out and decide for yourself. If you were an awakened soul, you would never have to ask for advice, you'd just listen to your intuition. Just know if you want career advice from a nurse, they'll tell you to be a nurse. If you ask a business advice from a sales person they'll tell you how to solve it with sales, not knowing accounting might be the problem. Just keep in mind that anyone you ask advice from is limited in what they know. Your best advisor is your intuition.

There are probably more personality types out there that are negative. If someone expresses a personality type it doesn't mean they're 100% negative, just be aware of how you're affected from being around them and don't stoop down to their level of energy. Keep yourself in a high vibrational frequency by keeping positive emotions.

A lot of people might have pieces of negative traits in them. As long as you are aware of them, you can start making changes. You'll have to do negative thought stopping in order for you to start making changes.

Avoid Reacting to Negative People or You'll Be One

After knowing what thoughts are negative, you need to understand how to stop yourself from thinking negative thoughts. Some may call it interrupting the pattern, or just plain old negative thought stopping, but I like to call it replacing darkness with light. Darkness is just the absence of light; negative thoughts is just the absence of positive thoughts.

There are negative people in our lives and I'll help you to deal with them, but the number one thing that affects you the most is your own negative thoughts. Just know that it's not negative people that's the problem. If you think "negative people are the problem!" They're never the problem. The problem is how you choose to react to negative people. If you negatively on auto-pilot, it means your consciously asleep.

It's time to wake up and know that negative people, circumstances and events only have power over you if you allow them to get under your skin. One of the greatest things to do is don't react to negative people. Start with your thought. If you decide to spend your energy reacting to negative people in a negative way, you're wasting energy and thought, that can be positive.

You can only feel one feel good or bad each moment of your life. If you choose to feel bad because you choose to react negatively towards someone, then you lost. If you react negatively to negative people, you just become one of them. It's a double loss, because your reacting negatively to them, and then after you blame them for your reaction. So, you might feel angry, and then you blame. Then you go into a negative spiral and it will take force and more energy to find a way to think positive again.

So, one of the best things to do is don't react at all. Which means change the subject, change what you're thinking. One of the ways to change what you're thinking is affirmations; another one just changes your focus. Think of people you love, think of your plans and goals. Your dominant thoughts in your mind should be everything you love, and your goals. If some how you go online and read bad news, then you react, and even worse, you share it. That's reacting, and you become one, with this negative news.

If someone is rude to you, or not nice to you. No matter who they are, there's really no need to be rude back. That's why Jesus got slapped in the face and didn't slap back. Buddha let the angry guy yell at him and said "If I refuse to receive a gift, who keeps it?" The person holding the gift. "If I refuse to accept your anger, who keeps it?" The person who tries to give you anger or hatred will keep that hatred multiplied times two. That hatred will destroy them as long as you refuse to react to it. So, keep yourself at peace with peaceful thoughts. Never connect with negative people by reacting to them.

Never let a negative person be worth your breath. Once you say their names you connect with the negative side of them. You also have will end up in a negative mood when you start talking about how you were wronged, how bad they are towards you, and how bad they make you feel. You end up becoming negative just by saying their name. If you must say it, say it fast and finish quickly without producing negative emotions.

Don't allow negative people to take space in your mind as well. When you let a negative person or situation to take space in your mind, you're giving it energy that you can be using for something productive. You can be using that energy to think of people you love, to imagine the life you want. One of the most common blockages in people's ability to get what they want and deserve in life is because they spend time and energy on what they don't want, and think of people they don't like.

Imagine if you think of someone who did you wrong. There would be a lot of negative possibilities that would happen in your mind. The greatest thing you can do at this point is to forgive, and send them love. The most common thing people do is reason out how bad they are, reaffirm how bad the person and situation are.

The second most common thing is they think of how to get back at that person who did them wrong. This will be in a form of revenge. This revenge will usually start by saying the person's name to other people and talking about how bad that person is. Trying to ruin the person's reputation and credibility to others. So, this is bad because you end up speaking with ill intentions.

The other option you'll have is to try to sabotage the person in some way. This is a bit worse cause what energy you give to the world will come back to you. Anytime you take action to try to sabotage someone, a day will come that you will be sabotaged. Also, by creating an energy of sabotage in your mind, body and soul, you will end up sabotaging yourself in some way. Even after you get your revenge, you'll definitely have bad karma so you'll be worried. If you lack the understanding of Karma, you'll definitely understand guilt.

Every Moment of Life is a Prayer

Every moment of life is a prayer. This is what I believe, and even religions say God see's all things all the time. So, if God see's all things all the time, then in a deeper sense, we're always connected to God. If we're always connected to God, even when not praying, every moment of life is a prayer. This is why it's important to be consciously aware of your emotions, thoughts and intentions. Your action always springs from within.

The quality of your thoughts and emotions determines the quality of your actions. When you have good quality actions, you have good quality effects. Any action we take while feeling good, has good consequences. Although there will be actions you take that feel good at the moment, but you know is not the right thing to do. Like cheating, one of the most common pleasurable acts that has negative consequences. It ruins your inner peace even if you don't get caught. Ruins your relationship if you do get caught.

If You Just Want the Summary Read Here

Everything that you want in life is really up to you. You have the power to be, do and have anything in the world. The problem is most of us, especially in the Philippines are surrounded by people with poverty mentality, limited knowledge of the world, people who have lack of self-belief, so it's impossible for them to believe in you. Most people have no knowledge of what's in this book. So, if more people know about ways to becoming successful then there would be more successful Filipinos.

Self-Image is one of the greatest obstacles we have in life.

While we're growing up, every around us shapes our self-image. We believe that whatever people say about us is correct. So, if someone says we're clumsy we'll occasionally drop things. If we lose in a sporting event, we think we're not athletic. As you grow older, realize that you have the power now to create yourself image. You can shape yourself image with the tools that has been written in this book, or if you need further coaching feel free to contact me.

Negative Beliefs should be a crime now. Eliminate negative beliefs about money, about relationships, about your potential, and about the world in general. Get rid of the beliefs that the world is scarce and your poor because those people are rich, they have all the money. Your negative beliefs about your health, that your genes are cancer prone. Anything you believe you create in your life. All negative beliefs can be easily replaced.

Everything that comes into your life is a result of your thought, feelings and actions. Whatever comes in your life tomorrow is the what you're thinking and feeling now. If you don't have the life you want then you need to change your thoughts, feelings and actions. It's all about your dominating thoughts and emotions. If you're thinking positive sometimes, but mostly negative then you're not going to attract much positive things. Stay aware of your dominating thoughts, feelings and actions and change them in a positive way to get positive results.

You have unlimited potential. A lot of people are stuck saying the story of their limitations. As an example, look at me. I continue to do what I want in life. Any skill that I'm interested to work on or business industry I want to get my hands on I go for it. Since I believe everything can be learned I learned to the point of getting paid in these things.

Stand-up comedy, screenwriting, music, poetry, writing books that are fiction and non-fiction, public speaking and keynote speaking, I have a furniture business, I have a training business, I make money teaching Yoga, business consultation and book sales, I sold motivational art, fresh water pearls, had a photography and music studio. I didn't even mention my digital marketing company, and the skills I possess and use in digital marketing, where train and do consultation. I'm doing all of these things at a high level. I'm currently getting paid or got paid for doing all of the things I just mentioned.

I believe I have unlimited potential; I just know that I haven't fully unlocked it because I have some bad habits that include drinking alcohol. But when I get in the zone in learning and working, it's like nothing can stop me. I have to finish certain projects; I have to reach certain goals in business and in life. I'm a C student in school, I always knew I didn't need school to succeed, but for sure we need to learn whatever skill or craft we want to be good at. I have an abundance of learning resources from my collection of 600 books, audio programs and online courses. You also need to find out where you can learn what you need to learn to achieve what you need to achieve.

Whatever you want in life, start the day with gratitude and positive expectation. These are really the two secrets of living a successful and happy life. If you continuously choose to feel grateful for every little thing in life and everything that has happened in your life that's good, you'll only receive what you feel in the future. The more grateful you are about your life, the more things that make you grateful appear.

When you expect good things in life, one the biggest benefits are you will eliminate worry doubt and fear. You can only feel good, or bad at each moment. So, it's either or. You can't feel good and bad at the same time. So, you fill your mind with thoughts and feelings of positive expectation than your more likely to manifest what you expect.

Sometimes we might have positive expectations about something but don't get what we expected. This can be because of contradicting thoughts of fear, doubt and worry. Also, you might have lacked confidence and competence. Positive expectation and visualization are good, but if you're not improving your skills and working on being the best at your craft or business then your just doing wishful thinking.

People need to also understand the law of compensation. You only get what you give in life. The amount of money you have right now is equal to the amount of value you've given to the world. If you want more money you need to give more value to more people, or higher quality value to more people. A lot of people work copy paste jobs, or are washing dishes and think they deserve to be a millionaire. Nothing wrong with those jobs, temporarily, but not for your whole life.

One way to make more money is really to provide higher quality value for your industry. If you are easily replaced then don't expect to make much money. If you are difficult to replace, like you're a Digital Marketer, who knows everything and more about digital marketing and can execute well. You're hard to find so you can demand higher pay. It's easy to find "Willing to be trained" workers or "Knows basic MS Word and Excel" but if you have a high paying skill, like Accounting, Marketing, Engineering, Graphic Designing, Video Editing, Copywriting, then you can get good money.

What high paying skill can you possess? Follow your passion. What high paying skill do you want to have? Figure that out, and then after that invest some money in learning it. Spend enough time each day to learn your skill and create products or services using your skill. Don't get stuck on looking for a job and asking your job to train you. No matter what job you have now, I'm sure you can spend 2 hours a day working on a skill that interests you and also provides high quality value the world is willing to pay big money for.

Continuously improve yourself. Every single day is a day to improve. Know that if your mind is filled with gossip and tv drama, you're probably not living a life you want to live. You might even be miserable. Improve the quality of your thoughts. Garbage in garbage out, so never fill your mind with useless information. Always ask yourself each day, how you can improve yourself. Let me ask you right now. How can you improve yourself today?

No matter what goal you have in life, just keep going for it. Never tell your goals to a pessimist or to someone you think isn't so smart. Never talk about your business ideas and do nothing about it. Instead when you talk to people, talk about your business progress. What progress have you had in your business idea? If you're stuck in this loop of seeing your friends every week end and talking about the same business idea. Stop embarrassing yourself and start working on it. If it's a lot of ideas choose the easiest one to work on.

Keep your intentions clean. Your intention to be successful, healthy or happy should be clean, it should be for other people, and to help others. Many people never get what they desire in life because they're intention to be rich is to make other people jealous, to say "I told you so" to whoever. Most people who want success to make others feel bad, seldom get it. Most people who have clean intentions to help others, always become successful if they put in the work. Pure intentions align you with God and you'll easily go from achieving one goal to another.

Continue to work out and feel good. Some people think that exercising isn't part of being successful. They eventually realize that working out and eating healthy is an essential part of happiness and wealth. The old saying Health is Wealth is absolutely true. A lot of people who start going the gym in their 40's and 50's is their because their doctor told them they have to start working out. Whatever age you are now its best if you start working out at least a couple of times a week.

I feel like the Philippines can one day be a First World Nation. So, this is part of my mission, it's to help the Philippines become a First World Nation. One way for me to do that is to educate as many Filipinos about their unlimited potential and help the achieve success through personal development training and Business Training.

I own a Business training Company and Digital Marketing Company, and we do training to help people improve their skills and in mostly everything in business and digital marketing. It can be management, supervisory, sales, digital marketing, accounting and more. I also do personal development training to help people reach their goals in business, money, happiness and health. If I can find a way to teach every Filipino how to enhance their business skills and personal development then it would be a good way to improve the country.

Another truth is our children are our future. So, I've always had this vision and plan that is starting to become clearer. It's to make a Charity that sponsors children to go to school and also provides food for them. I feel bad for those kids who say they stopped going to school because they have no money. Helping as many kids get education is my social responsibility. As for now I just do guerilla charity where I just give random kids like P500 or P1000. It's nice to be the person that gave them the most money they ever had. It has a short-term effect though. So, when I have enough funds, I'll start this charity to sponsor them to go to school, pay for food and give other bonusses.

Thank You so Much for Reading This Book. I hope you learned enough to apply what works for you to improve your life. Feel free to contact me at marqmartincom for questions, comments or inquiries.

Thanks Again

Made in the USA
Columbia, SC
03 October 2023

23870486R00090